Celebrating Passover

A Guide to Understanding the Jewish Passover for Latter-day Saints

Celebrating Passover

A Guide to Understanding the Jewish Passover for Latter-day Saints

Marianne Monson-Burton

First Printing, February, 2004

International Standard Book Number
0-88290-759-X

Horizon Publishers' Catalog and Order Number
H2101

Printed and distributed
in the United States of America by

Mailing Address:
925 North Main
Springville, Utah 84663

Phone and Fax:
Local Phone: (801) 489-4084
Toll Free: 1 (800) 759-2665
FAX: (801) 489-1097

www.cedarfort.com

Contents

Part One
Understanding Passover

Part Two
Celebrating a
Latter-day Saint Passover

Dedication

This book is dedicated with deepest gratitude
—to my parents, for their teachings,
—to my husband, Keith, for unfailing support,
—and to our children, Nathanael and Aria,
        for the wonders they show me each day.

Acknowledgments

I am indebted to the dedicated and talented scholars who taught me in Jerusalem, including Dr. M. Catherine Thomas, Dr. Brent L. Topp, Dr. Byron Merrill, and Dr. Donald Parry; with special thanks to Rabbi David Rosen, for sharing his beautiful religion with me; also to Dr. Victor L. Ludlow, who has shared the message of Passover with Latter-day Saints around the globe, and whose involvement with this project is deeply appreciated.

I am grateful to the editorial staff at Horizon Publishers for their vision, and especially to Duane S. and Jean D. Crowther, who shepherded the manuscript through the selection, editorial, typesetting and design processes with care.

Acknowledgement is owed to my mother, Marilynn Monson for sharing her recipes. Finally, gratitude is expressed to my family and friends who reviewed the manuscript in its earliest revisions, with special recognition of my husband, who has always believed in me and in this book.

Glossary and Pronunciation Guide for Hebrew Terms

Pronunciation Key

"a, ah" as in "father"	"e" as in "set"
"ay" as in "game"	"ee" as in "feet"
"o" as in "open"	"i" as in "die"
"oo" as in "food"	"I" as in "win"
"u" as in "funny"	"g" as in "gone"

"ch" represents the Hebrew letter "che." It represents a guttural sound not found in English, but it is similar to the French "R" and the consonant sound in the German word "ach."

Afikoman (*a-fee-KO-mun*): The portion of the unleavened bread that is broken and hidden during the Seder.

Beytzah (*bay-TZAH*): The roasted egg on the passover plate.

Charoset (*cha-RO-set*): A mixture of nuts, fruit, and honey on the Passover plate, recalling the mortar the Israelites made in Egypt.

Dayenu (*di-AY-noo*): "It would have been enough." Said as blessings are recounted during the Seder.

Gefilte Fish (*gu-FIL-tu*): A traditional fish dish.

Haggadah (*ha-ga-DAH*): "The telling." This is the name of the script read at the Passover dinner.

Karpas (*kar-PAS*): parsley or other green vegetable on the Passover plate.

Kiddush (*KID-oosh*): Blessing said over wine or bread to mark the beginning of Passover or Sabbath observance.

Potato Latkes (*LOHT-kuz*): Traditional potato pancakes.

Matzah (*MA-tzah*): Unleavened bread (singular). Plural is **Matzot** (*MA-tzot*).

Maror (*ma-ROR*): The horseradish or other bitter herb on the Passover plate.

Mishnah (*MISH-nah*): Collection of Jewish oral tradition compiled around 200 A.D.

Seder (*SAY-der*): The name for the Passover dinner, including the recitations and songs.

Talmud (*TAL-mood*): Authoritative body of Jewish tradition, including the Mishnah and Gemara.

Zeroah (*zeh-ro-AH*): "Forearm." name given to the lamb shank bone on the Passover plate.

Preface

The Passover—
Remembering Deliverance
and the Paschal Lamb

Victor L. Ludlow, BYU Professor of Ancient Scripture

When students of the scriptures think of the Passover, they usually connect with both Old and New Testament events. They recall the original Passover as the Lord commanded the Israelites to prepare for their exodus from Egypt. They also think of the Last Supper as Jesus celebrated the Passover prior to instituting the new ordinance of the sacrament. Thus, the Passover is an important time for remembering God and His deliverance from both physical and spiritual captivity.

In this short and helpful book by Marianne Monson-Burton, she guides us through both ancient traditions and modern applications of the Passover. She opens up the Passover as she provides historical background, gospel context, definitions of symbols, tasty recipes, and other resources for Latter-day Saints who not only want to know more about this ancient Biblical practice but also desire to incorporate elements of it into their Easter season.

When God first instituted the Passover, He stipulated strict guidelines governing the selection and manner of killing, cooking, and eating the Paschal Lamb. There was to be one lamb per household, with one household consisting of a familial patriarch and all his descendants. The Lord Himself gave the meaning of the Paschal Sacrifice. In the words of Moses,

It shall come to pass, when your children shall say unto you,
What mean ye by this service?

That ye shall say, It is the sacrifice of the Lord's
Passover, who passed over the houses of the children of
Israel in Egypt, when he smote the Egyptians, and delivered
our houses. And the people bowed their head and worshiped.[1]

It is thus clear that from the very origins of Passover, the
Paschal Sacrifice was to be the central focus. During the Second Temple Period (516 b.c.e. – 70 c.e.), it remained so and
was given even heightened significance as the tradition developed to perform the sacrifice only at the Temple in Jerusalem.
Several characteristics distinguish the Paschal Sacrifice from
other Temple sacrifices. For example, all other sacrifices at
the Temple were offered on behalf of an individual, but the
Paschal Sacrifice was offered on behalf of the group of people who would later partake of it. Also making this sacrifice
unique was that it was actually performed by the household
representative rather than the Levites at the Temple, albeit, the
Levites were always on hand to assist and ensure that the sacrifice was conducted properly. (Note in Luke 22:7-13 and
Mark 14:12-16 how Peter and John make the necessary
Passover preparations, including the Paschal Sacrifice, for the
Last Supper meal of Jesus and his apostles.)

These Passover requirements for sacrificing the Paschal
Lamb continued until the destruction of Jerusalem and the
Temple in 70 c.e., after which the Jews were unable to perform this important sacrifice. By this time, Christians had
already substituted the sacrament as a symbol of the Paschal
Sacrifice. Therefore, the actual sacrifice is no longer a part of
either Passover or Easter festivities, yet its essence lives on in
many ways. For contemporary Jewry, the Afikoman has come

_____

1. Exodus 12:26-27.

to replace or represent the Paschal Lamb, in the sense that it is the last thing eaten during the Seder of Passover night. Also, the essence of the Paschal Sacrifice lies at the heart of Christendom as the followers of Jesus remember His atoning sacrifice as the Lamb of God.

In this book, Marianne Monson-Burton helps us connect with both the physical experiences and the spiritual symbols of the Paschal Sacrifice. Reading and applying the insights from *Celebrating Passover* will enrich the Easter experience for Latter-day Saints who desire to remember and celebrate God's deliverance of His children through His Son, Jesus Christ.

VLL

Introduction

For the past ten years I have had the honor of sharing a Latter-day Saint's view of Passover in lessons, Sacrament Meeting talks, firesides, and family celebrations. After one such evening, a friend wrote, "We loved learning the meaning and history behind the traditional Jewish holiday. We reread about Christ and Passover in the Gospels after our dinner with you and felt amazed by the depth of understanding we had gained."[1] Over years of research and celebration, I have grown to love this holiday that inevitably draws participants closer to Christ.

My first experience with Passover occurred as a student at BYU's Jerusalem Center for Near Eastern Studies. I arrived there as a freshman, with very little knowledge of Jerusalem's history and politics. For six months I was flooded with information, experiences, and spiritual growth. I fell in love with the cultures that share the land of Israel/Palestine. Deeply inspired by the sincere religious devotion of my Muslim and Jewish teachers, I gained a deep, abiding respect for both religions. Our Jewish teacher was Rabbi David Rosen, and I will never forget the reverence with which he taught us about Judaism. Through his words the ancient religion (which shares a common history with my own) came alive for me. Suddenly, the Old Testament was full of insightful depths and a gentle power I had never comprehended before.

Shortly before Easter, we were invited to join Rabbi Rosen and his family in celebrating the Passover Seder. I watched in awe as he and his wife lovingly blessed their children, lit

---

1. Melinda Wolfer, letter to author, April 2001.

candles, broke bread, and sang songs of devotion. Rabbi Rosen's reverence for the ceremony touched me deeply, and the spirit testified of truth. Later, as I pondered the scriptures and the service I had witnessed, I became convinced that Passover symbolized the atonement of Christ. I was deeply moved by the experience and yearned to keep the celebration with my own family. But I wondered if I could, appropriately, celebrate Passover as a member of The Church of Jesus Christ of Latter-day Saints.

Just a few days after Passover, I spent Easter at the garden tomb, reading the resurrection accounts, praying, and communing with God. The Easter lilies were radiantly silver and fragrant; the garden was bursting with life. I felt the Savior's presence so near, it seemed that my prayers were simply conversations with someone who sat beside me. I stood with a friend inside the tomb and looked out at the glorious garden. In reverent whispers we asked each other: "What would we have seen if we were standing in this spot two thousand years ago?" Tears filled our eyes as we imagined Mary entering the garden, grieving, then returning as the first witness of the resurrected Lord. At that moment, the years seemed to fall away and I felt that I was there as it happened.

After returning home, I reflected on this profound Easter experience. I realized that the holiday celebrating the resurrection of Christ is truly the most important day of the year—and an annual opportunity to reflect upon the gift of spiritual freedom bought by the Savior. I determined to make future Easters more meaningful and focused on Christ, and I realized that celebrating a Latter-day Saint's version of Passover could help. As I continued my research, I learned that this idea is not without historical precedence, for that is exactly how Easter was originally kept. In the earliest years following the resurrection of Jesus, the apostles and other Christians gathered to observe a Passover festival focused on Jesus, the holy Lamb of God. They called this holiday "Pascha." Eventually the holiday was renamed "Easter" and moved further away from its Jewish roots.[2]

Every year since that experience in Jerusalem, I have gathered with family and friends to observe the Passover feast as part of our Easter celebration. Passover has become one of our family's most important traditions. Every year the service is slightly different because we adjust the length and focus to fit the age and interests of participants, but every year I find a new way of looking at the symbolism that brings me closer to my Savior. I marvel at the Lord's wisdom in creating a holy day that reveals the Atonement as the moment of liberation for all mankind.

Inevitably, participants at our Passover meal want to know where to find more information on Passover from a Latter-day Saint perspective. While there are many books on Passover for the mainstream Christian market, this is the first book to examine it specifically from an LDS view.

The goal of this book is to give an introduction to the wealth of spiritual insight found in the feast of Passover. The first half of the book includes an introduction to the Passover feast, a look at how it has changed over the years, and an explanation of how the festival symbols point to Christ. The second half of the book provides Latter-day Saint readers with all of the information and tools necessary to celebrate a version of the holiday in their own homes, and also includes recipes and preparation tips. Chapter 10 is a Mormon interpretation of the Haggadah, the script read at Passover dinner.

---

2. As discussed in Chapter 3.

It is important to realize that I am not in any way suggesting that keeping Passover is required, nor that it should become a mainstream practice in the Church. Passover is simply an ancient holy day that symbolizes the Lord's atonement. Celebrating it from a Latter-day Saint perspective can teach us truths, offer insights into the life of Christ, and may become a meaningful tradition for families. But, of course, when all is said and done, the law of Moses has been fulfilled with the coming of the Savior in the Meridian of time.[3] Today we have been commanded to partake of the Sacrament as the central act of our worship services.[4]

Nonetheless, studying and celebrating Passover has greatly blessed my life. When I study Passover, I gain new insights about my Savior and the prophecies of His coming. My hope is that this book will give you the inspiration and resources to use the Passover in your life—in talks, in lessons, and above all, in your family. May it bring you closer to the Lord who instituted it, celebrated it, and lovingly fulfilled it.

This is my prayer.

—Marianne Monson-Burton

---

3. 3 Ne. 9:16-20; 15:2-9; 2 Ne. 25:24-25; D&C 22:1-4; Mt. 5:17-18; Jn. 1:17; Ro. 10:4-6; Gal. 3:13-29; 4:3-5; 5:1-6.

4. Mt. 26:26-27; Jn. 6:53-58; 1 Cor. 11:23-29; Morm. 9:29; 3 Ne. 18:5-12; D&C 59:9; 62:4.

Part 1

Understanding Passover

1
Why Would a Latter-day Saint Celebrate Passover?

Since the beginning of time, God has extended invitations designed to focus the easily forgetful human heart on the life, mission and atoning sacrifice of our Lord. It is human nature to lapse into spiritual complacency when life is peaceful and prosperous, regardless of good intentions. Like the children of Israel who witnessed the miracle of the Red Sea, it is all too easy to return to our own golden calves, abandoning the God we love. But as Elder Henry B. Eyring has taught, "There seems to be no end to the Savior's desire to lead us to safety. And there is constancy in the way He shows us the path. He calls by more than one means so that it will reach those willing to accept it."[1]

With infinite patience He has provided a multitude of reminders to call us back to the gospel feast. He taught our first parents, Adam and Eve, about the importance of calling on God's name in prayer. To the children of Israel, He gave the tabernacle with its ritual sacrifices to keep them in constant remembrance. To the disciples in Jesus' day, He gave the sacrament. And today, in this final dispensation, the Lord has showered us with truth found in scripture, temple covenants, and sacred ordinances. Every one of these divine invitations has been revealed through a prophet for the purpose of calling us to belief, faith and adoration of God the Father and His Only Begotten Son in the flesh, our Lord Jesus Christ. Truly

---

1. Henry B. Eyring, "Finding Safety in Counsel," *Ensign*, May 1997, 24.

our Heavenly Father is a God of endless mercy! Not only did He provide the world with the atoning sacrifice of His beloved Son, but He then extended a multitude of invitations to draw us to the Savior's loving arms.

Passover is one of many "invitations" that God extended to His people in ancient times. Instituted by the Lord through the prophet Moses, Passover has been kept sacred by Israelites and their descendants for thousands of years. Through symbolism, this feast prepared them for the coming of a Savior. Passover pointed them toward the Lord's atoning sacrifice He would make in behalf of all mankind, yet it still has much to teach us today. When the Savior appeared to the Nephites after his resurrection, he reminded them that commandments and symbols of the former covenant still contained great value. He said, "Ye ought to search these things. Yea, a commandment I give unto you that ye search these things diligently."[2]

In addition to its role in ancient times, Passover has continued to play a part in important gospel events, such as the institution of the sacrament and the restoration of the sealing keys. The history of this feast is woven through the fabric of the gospel—from the time of Moses to the restoration of the Church in the days of Joseph Smith. Passover is even connected with the Book of Mormon and the Second Coming of the Savior. As a symbol of the Atonement, the lessons to be learned from the Passover feast are vast. Elder Bruce R. McConkie once said, "Everything connected with the Passover period is so dramatic, so filled with symbolism, so designed to center the attention of the Lord's people in the great eternal truths of salvation, that even today, when the

---

2. 3 Nephi 23:1.

Passover is past and we no longer need, to the extent our fore-
bears did, to ponder its place in the plan of salvation, we are
still prone to use its happenings to teach various related truths
and principles."[3]

The Lord instituted Passover to be celebrated by God's
children annually. The Lord told Moses, "[Passover] is that
night of the Lord to be observed of all the children of Israel in
all their generations. Therefore shall ye observe this day in
your generations by an ordinance for ever"[4] Four times in that
chapter the Lord said that Passover is supposed to be a
covenant forever. That's right—God said *forever,* not just
until the law was fulfilled. In fact, Passover was instituted
before the Mosaic Law was even given. On the surface, these
scriptures may seem confusing to Latter-day Saints. If
Passover is an eternal commandment, then why don't we
observe it as part of the restored gospel?

The reassuring answer is that we do celebrate the eternal
feast of Passover when we celebrate Easter and partake of the
sacrament, because more importantly, we celebrate all that
Passover prepared the world to experience. In actuality, Easter and Passover are the same holiday. Passover celebrates
physical freedom bought with the blood of a sacrificial lamb.
Easter celebrates spiritual freedom bought with the blood of
the sinless Lamb of God. Thousands of years before our Savior's birth, our Father designed a way for the children of
Israel to physically experience a symbol of the spiritual miracle we all need: release from bitter bondage because of the
sacrifice of God's holy Lamb. As President Howard W.
Hunter taught, "Passover is linked with the Christian observance of Easter. . . . The Passover in the Old Testament and

---

3. Bruce R. McConkie, *The Mortal Messiah: From Bethlehem to
Calvary* (Salt Lake City: Deseret Books, 1980), 1:165.
    4. Exodus 12:42, 17.

Easter in the New Testament testify of the great gift God has given and of the sacrifice that was involved in its bestowal. Both of these great religious commemorations declare that death would 'pass over' us and could have no permanent power upon us, and that the grave would have no victory."[5]

As Latter-day Saints, we celebrate Easter and believe that the Mosaic Law does not need to be observed any longer, but there are several reasons why Passover can still play an important role in a Mormon home today.

A Christ-centered Easter

First, Easter is the holiest day of the year. Christmas gets a lot of attention, but technically we wouldn't celebrate the Savior's birth if not for his death and resurrection. In spite of this, even families who have customs that focus on the true meaning of Christmas sometimes find it difficult to impart the real message of Easter to their children. Between the Easter Bunny and candy egg hunts, many children (and adults) miss the opportunity of allowing this holiday to strengthen their understanding of the Atonement. "Easter is a sacred day, a day of thanksgiving and divine worship," President David O. McKay once said. "It is not a day just for rejoicing because of the opening of springtime; it is an occasion for the expression of gratitude to God for having sent His Only Begotten Son into the world to be 'the way, the truth, the life.'"[6] Creating Easter activities that reflect President McKay's words is a challenge for all LDS families. Celebrating an LDS version of

_____

5. Howard W. Hunter, "Christ, Our Passover," *Ensign,* May 1985, 17.

6. As quoted in Ann H. Banks, "Family Easter Traditions," *Ensign,* April 1982, 12.

Passover can begin a family tradition that focuses the attention of Easter back where it belongs—on Christ.

Teach It to Your Children

Second, Passover was created for families. The holiday is to be celebrated in a family setting, with the specific goal of teaching children about the compassion and power of God. Exodus reads, "It shall come to pass, when your children shall say unto you, 'What mean ye by this service?' that ye shall say, 'It is the sacrifice of the Lord's passover, who passed over the houses of the children of Israel in Egypt when he . . . delivered our houses.'"[7] The primary goal of Passover is to teach younger generations about the deliverance of the Lord. Although aspects of the celebration have changed through the centuries, it has remained true to this purpose. Through Passover, children learn to liken the scriptures to their own lives, for Passover testifies that even as the Lord redeemed our ancestors, He redeems us as well. Children are involved in the ceremony; they ask questions, read scriptures, and go on a "treasure hunt" for the afikoman. Passover is an opportunity for youth of all ages to learn about the prophecies of Christ. It binds generations together in a celebration of spiritual freedom.

The Lord's Holy Day

Third, Passover was divinely instituted. As God of the Old Testament, Jesus Christ established Passover as a symbol of his future atoning sacrifice. The Mosaic Law symbolized Christ, and prepared the Earth for his coming. We know that the Nephites observed the Law of Moses with this understanding. Amulek taught, "Behold, this is the whole meaning

---

7. Exodus 12:26-27.

of the law, every whit pointing to that great and last sacrifice; and that great and last sacrifice will be the Son of God, yea infinite and eternal."[8] Although the law has been fulfilled, it is not without value for us today. The Lord has commanded, "Remember the former things of old: I am God and there is none like me, declaring the end from the beginning and from ancient times the things that are not yet done, . . . yea, I have spoken it, I will also bring it to pass."[9] The more we learn about the prophecies of Christ, the more we understand and appreciate their fulfillment. By studying God's commands in every age, we learn that the course of the Lord is one eternal round.

Throughout Gospel History

Fourth, Passover has played a crucial role in many sacred events best understood in the original context of this festival. Elements of Passover are woven throughout the miracles and teachings of Jesus. It was the Savior himself who established the link between Passover and his own sacrifice; He used the traditional Passover symbols of unleavened bread and wine to teach the disciples about his upcoming sacrifice when he instituted the sacrament. Later, the celebration of Easter actually began as a Christian version of Passover. During the restoration of the Gospel in the dispensation of the fulness of times, Elijah returned to the Kirtland Temple on Passover in fulfillment of Jewish prophecies. There are even connections between Passover and the Book of Mormon, as well as the Second Coming of the Lord. Studying Passover sheds light on a myriad of related gospel truths, for the miracles of former days foreshadow events of future latter-day events.

---

8. Alma 34:14.
9. Isaiah 46:9-11.

Truly, the Passover celebration has much to teach us. Passover symbolism is rich and multifaceted. It is simple enough to teach to a child, yet deep enough to awe the greatest gospel scholar with the wisdom and mercy of God. The lessons to be learned from it are inexhaustible, because it is inseparably connected with the Atonement of our Savior. As LDS author Terry W. Treseder expressed, "The more we understand and appreciate the Passover service . . . the more deeply we can understand our sacramental covenants and marvel anew at the infinite love and patience of our Brother, the Lord Jesus Christ."[10] This is a goal to occupy a lifetime and into eternity.

---

10. Terry W. Treseder, "Passover Promises Fulfilled in the Last Supper," *Ensign*, April 1990, 19.

2
What Is Passover?

To appreciate the origins of Passover, one must return to a time thousands of years ago, when the children of Israel were slaves in Egypt. As members of The Church of Jesus Christ of Latter-day Saints, we consider these men and women our literal ancestors, for as patriarchal blessings witness, the great majority of church members are from the tribe of Ephraim and those who are not literal descendants are grafted into the house of Israel at the time of their baptism.[1] Genealogically, we share a common blood line with the Jews, for we are all descendants of Abraham and Israel. The Passover story should be familiar to us, for it holds special relevance to modern Israel.

The First Passover in Egypt

Our ancestors' captivity began when Jacob's sons sold their brother Joseph into slavery. Joseph trusted in God, and through the timely use of revelation, his fortunes were reversed and he became an important counselor to Pharaoh. While food was plentiful, God inspired Joseph to store rations for difficult times ahead. The foretold famine struck, and Joseph's brothers journeyed from Israel to Egypt seeking sustenance for their family. When Joseph and his brothers were reunited, Jacob and the remaining family members joined them in Egypt. As the years passed, Jacob's posterity multiplied and prospered.

---

1. Joseph F. Smith, *Doctrines of Salvation: Sermons and Writings of Joseph Fielding Smith* (Salt Lake City: Bookcraft, 1992), 3:246.

Eventually Jacob and Joseph passed away, and after many years "there arose up a new king over Egypt."[2] This Pharaoh did not remember Joseph's contribution. He saw the thriving population of Israelites as a threat to his power, so he enslaved them. The scriptures record, "Therefore they did set over them taskmasters to afflict them with their burdens. And they made their lives bitter with hard bondage."[3] In spite of captivity, God blessed the Israelites and their numbers continued to increase. When Pharaoh saw the Israelites growing stronger in spite of bondage, he issued a horrifying decree: the midwives were commanded to kill every newborn Israelite male.

At this agonizing time, a righteous Levite woman named Jochebed gave birth to a son. Fearing for his life, she hid him for three months, but unable to conceal the growing baby, she sealed an ark made of bulrushes, placed her son inside, and left the ark at the river's edge, where Pharaoh's daughter bathed. When the Egyptian Princess opened the ark and realized that an anguished Hebrew mother had set the crying baby adrift, her heart was moved with compassion. The baby's sister stood nearby and offered to bring a Hebrew woman to nurse the child, then returned with Jochebed. So the baby was nursed by his own mother but raised as an Egyptian prince. Pharaoh's daughter named him Moses, which means "to draw out," because she had drawn him out of the water. Little could she dream the name also foretold his role as a Prophet who would draw his people out of bondage.

When Moses grew to adulthood, he began to recognize the burden of captivity resting on his people. One day when

2. Exodus 1:8.
3. Exodus 1:11,14.

he saw an Egyptian taskmaster beating a Hebrew, Moses was filled with indignation. He interfered to save the slave, and in the process Moses killed the Egyptian taskmaster. When the crime became known, Pharaoh "sought to slay Moses,"[4] so Moses fled Egypt and took refuge in Midian, on the modern-day Sinai Peninsula. There he met the priest Jethro and married his daughter, Zipporah. Moses "was content" and would have been happy to remain a humble shepherd with his father-in-law, but the Lord had a different plan for him.[5] God had heard the mournful prayers of the Israelites, and He remembered the covenant He had made with their fathers. One day as Moses tended his flock near mount Sinai he saw an eerie sight. Upon the mountainside, a "bush burned with fire and the bush was not consumed."[6] As he went closer to investigate, the voice of God called to him from the fiery shrub and, in one of the greatest recorded moments of theophany, Moses was instructed, "I have surely seen the affliction of my people which are in Egypt and have heard their cry . . . and I am come down to deliver them."[7]

God commanded Moses to go before Pharaoh and demand the freedom of His people. Moses was shocked. How could he, a lowly shepherd who fled Egypt as a fugitive, make requirements of the mighty Pharaoh? He protested, "Who am I that I should go? I am slow of speech and of a slow tongue."[8] Moses did not yet understand that the talent of one who stands with God does not matter because the Lord Himself guides and guards the work. God replied, "Who hath made man's

---

4. Exodus 2:15.
5. Exodus 2:21.
6. Exodus 3:2.
7. Exodus 3:7-8.
8. Exodus 3:11, 4:10.

mouth? Have not I the Lord? Therefore go, and I will teach thee what thou shalt say. I will stretch out my hand, and smite Egypt with all my wonders."[9]

So Moses went. With his brother Aaron, he appeared before Pharaoh and boldly proclaimed, "Thus saith the Lord God of Israel, 'Let my people go.'"[10] Pharaoh responded brashly, "Who is the Lord that I should obey his voice? I know not the Lord, neither will I let Israel go."[11] Instead of granting freedom, Pharaoh increased the burdens placed on Israel, so the Lord commanded Moses to smite Egypt that Pharaoh's heart might be humbled.

Plagues rained down in rapid succession: the river was turned to blood, frogs spread upon the land, lice pestered both man and beast, flies swarmed, cattle died of plague, and horrible boils afflicted the Egyptians. Eventually, hail and fire fell from the sky, locusts devoured the crops, and for three days total darkness covered the land. During the height of each plague, Pharaoh agreed to let Israel go worship in the wilderness. Then, as soon as the Lord removed each curse, Pharaoh hardened his heart and refused to let them go.

The Lord had been patient with Pharaoh. Moses had clearly explained the consequences for Egypt's obstinacy. Now the time had come for one final plague so horrific even Pharaoh would be forced to relent. The Lord said, "Israel is my son, even my firstborn . . . if thou refuse to let him go, behold I will slay thy son, even thy firstborn."[12] The final plague was thus identified.

---

9. Exodus 4:11-12; 3:20.
10. Exodus 5:1.
11. Exodus 5:2.
12. Exodus 4:22-23.

In preparation for this ultimate plague, the Lord gave detailed instructions to Moses. In order to spare their righteous posterity, each Israelite family was commanded to choose a perfect male lamb. The lamb was slaughtered and a branch of hyssop was used to paint the blood on the top and sides of the doorframe. That night they roasted the lamb and ate it with bitter herbs and unleavened bread; they ate in haste, prepared to leave at any moment. As night fell over Egypt, the Israelites remained in their homes marked with the lamb blood, for the Lord had commanded them to stay inside. At midnight, the land of Egypt was silent and dark. Perhaps the light of a full moon glinted on the red, bloodstained doorposts as the Lord sent a destroying angel through the land of Egypt.[13] In every Egyptian household, the destroying angel killed the firstborn of both man and beast. But the angel of death passed over every Israelite home marked with the blood of the lamb. Because the token of blood set them apart, Israelite families were spared the plague of death, and this night of deliverance became the first Passover.

But the night of miracles was also filled with horror. A great and awful cry rang through Egypt "for there was not a house where there was not one dead."[14] Grief-stricken, Pharaoh called Moses and Aaron to him while it was still night. He told them to take their people and leave before the land of Egypt was destroyed completely. So the children of Israel gathered their children, flocks, and possessions and

---

13. The Passover occurred on the 15th of Nisan. Because the Jewish calendar is lunar, this date always falls on a full moon. See Ira Steingroot, *Keeping Passover: Everything You Need to Know to Bring the Ancient Tradition to Life and Create Your Own Passover Celebration* (San Francisco: HarperCollins, 1995), 17.

14. Exodus 12:30.

started on their flight. They left behind the bitterness of servitude and embarked on a journey toward the Promised Land. A cloud led them through the wilderness by day and a pillar of fire watched over them at night. The vast power of God was demonstrated on their behalf as the Red Sea parted, allowing them to walk through on dry ground. As they walked, they sang and rejoiced. After almost three hundred years, Joseph's posterity finally journeyed in freedom![15]

To fully understand the significance of Passover, we must remember that this day marks the birth of the Israelite nation. Previously they were merely slaves to a greater nation. Now God had called them to be separate and free. Israel was set up as a nation, unique in the entire world—God was its Sovereign and a Prophet was its leader. This government was the first Theocracy.

A Covenant For Ever

To commemorate deliverance from bondage, the Lord required Israelites to celebrate the anniversary of their redemption annually. The day after Passover, the Feast of Unleavened Bread began, and no leaven (yeast) could be eaten during this time. The perpetual holiday was an opportunity to instruct children concerning the miraculous liberation. The Lord commanded Israel to celebrate this holy day forever: "This day shall be unto you for a memorial; and ye shall keep it a feast to the Lord throughout your generations; ye shall keep it a feast by an ordinance for ever."[16] The day was

---

15. Scholars estimate that the time in Egypt was approximately 1550-1280 B.C. See Barry L. Bandstra, *Reading the Old Testament: An Introduction to the Hebrew Bible* (Belmont, WA: Wadsworth Publishing, 1995), 13.

16. Exodus 12:14.

of such monumental importance that God even instructed the Israelites to begin their calendar year with the month of the Passover miracle. It is astounding that this ancient holiday is still reverently observed after more than three thousand years.[17]

Today, Passover is often called the Freedom Festival because it celebrates the deliverance of God's people in every age. If God had not brought our ancestors out of Egypt, we would still be slaves. In essence, on that day God released all of us. As the Jews say at Passover, "In every generation, each of us should feel as though we ourselves had gone forth from Egypt."[18] Each time God releases his people—from Babylon, from the Crusades, or from concentration camps—it is seen as a continuation of the Passover epic.

Passover and Easter

From the LDS perspective, Jehovah, the pre-mortal Jesus and God of the Old Testament, originally instituted the Passover festival as a symbol of his own atoning sacrifice. Passover symbols were fulfilled through the Atonement, when God said a second time, "I have surely seen the affliction of my people and have heard their cry . . . and I am come down to deliver them."[19] Christ is the holy lamb whose blood allows us to be "passed over" by the destroying angel. Because of his sacrifice, we are released from the bondage of sin and death. We celebrate his triumph at Easter, which is another freedom festival: a time of rejoicing and gratitude for the deliverance from death and sin made possible through the

17. Scholars estimate the Exodus at 1280 B.C. See Bandstra, 13.

18. Herbert Bronstein and Leonard Baskin, *A Passover Haggadah* (New York: The Central Conference of American Rabbis, 1994), 56.

19. Exodus 3:7, 8.

mercy of God. As Nephi taught, "The Messiah cometh in the fullness of time, that he may redeem the children of men from the fall and because that they are redeemed from the fall, they have become free forever."[20]

In a very real sense, Passover and Easter are the same holiday. Passover simply looked forward in anticipation of the Atonement, while Easter looks back in commemoration. President Howard W. Hunter said, "I believe it is safe to say that Passover is without equal in the Jewish calendar of celebrations. It commemorates the passage of a people from subjection and bondage to freedom and deliverance. Passover in the Old Testament and Easter in the New Testament testify of the great gift God has given and of the sacrifice that was involved in its bestowal."[21]

Passover Today

Today the Passover holiday is observed for eight days outside of Israel.[22] During these eight days, only unleavened bread is eaten and nothing made with yeast is permitted in the home. The first two days and the last two days are holy—they are observed according to Sabbath law, for Jews consider them "extra Sabbaths."

On the first two nights of the holiday, a special service called the Seder[23] is observed. The Seder is a retelling of the Exodus story in a dramatic pageant, enacted by a family and

---

20. 2 Nephi 2:27.

21. Hunter, "Christ, Our Passover," 17.

22. Passover lasts seven days in Israel. Most Jewish holidays are observed for one extra day outside of Israel, a tradition dating from times when slow communication made it impossible for Jews outside of Israel to know the exact start of holidays, since it was determined by sighting the new moon in Jerusalem.

23. Pronounced SAY-der.

its guests around a festive table. There are spoken parts for children and adults, chorus recitations and songs, and a variety of colorful food symbols, all of which assist in telling the freedom story.

Scripts and directions used in conducting a Seder are recorded in a book called the Haggadah,[24] a Hebrew word that means, "the telling." Thousands of Haggadahs are available today, and while each retains the same basic structure, portions are tailored for the intended audience. For instance, some Haggadahs are directed at families with young children, and some are tailored for women, while others focus on the Holocaust. Still other Haggadahs present a Christian version of the ceremony. Chapter 10 of this book is a retelling of the Haggadah from the LDS perspective. Although it is essentially a traditional Jewish Haggadah, commentary and interpretations have been adapted for an LDS audience.

Despite variations, the basic Haggadah remains the same. This remarkable book is actually a collage of four thousand years of Jewish life, literature, and tradition. The Haggadah is a brilliant mosaic made up of scripture, theological questions, poems, folk songs, and prayers—influenced by a vast array of Jewish experience spread over a multitude of lands and centuries of time. Poetry from the time of King David is placed alongside scripture from the Babylonian exile and rabbinic writings from the Middle Ages. Even some of the rabbis' ancient jokes are woven in!

Somehow the compilation as a whole contains a power and beauty far greater than any individual part. As one Jewish scholar observed, "The fact that it is cryptic or disjointed has little to do with its ability to work its magic on us. When we

---

24. Pronounced ha-ga-DAH.

participate in the reading of the Haggadah, we become heir to this resonant, multilayered tradition of Jewish life and learning. As the sages said of the [Bible], 'Turn it and turn it again, for everything is in it.'"[25]

The Modern Seder

An overview of the Seder as found in modern Haggadahs is shown here.

Opening: Welcome guests and sanctify the day. Light the candles, offer a prayer.

First cup: Pour the first cup of wine (or grape juice).[26]

Wash hands: Pass a bowl of water for washing hands.

Karpas:[27] Eat a green leafy vegetable, such as parsley.

Conceal afikoman:[28] Three pieces of unleavened bread are on the table. Break the middle piece, wrap it in a napkin, and hide it somewhere in the house.

Narration: The youngest child asks questions about the meal. Sing a song to explain why this night is different from all other nights. Tell the Exodus story.

The "Dayenu"[29] ***song:*** A song reminds the guests about the gifts the Lord has given. After each blessing participants say, "Dayenu," or "it would have been enough for us."

---

25. Steingroot, *op. cit.,* 116.
26. Four cups of wine are consumed throughout the Jewish Seder. Each cup is dedicated to one of the four promises in Exodus 6:6-7. In this book, it is assumed that the reader will prefer to use grape juice, in keeping with the LDS Word of Wisdom. This is an acceptable deviation and many health-conscious Jews today do the same.
27. Pronounced kar-PAS.
28. Pronounced a-fee-KO-mun.
29. Pronounced di-AY-noo.

Symbolism discussed: Explain the special food symbols on the Passover plate.

Second cup: Pour the second cup of grape juice.

Matzah:[30] Bless and eat the unleavened bread.

Maror:[31] Bless and eat bitter herbs, such as horseradish. Then dip the bitter herb in a sweet sauce called charoset[32] and eat again.

Meal: Bless, serve, and eat the meal.

Prayers: Offer prayers of gratitude.

Find afikoman: The children search for the hidden bread wrapped in a napkin. They bring it to the table and receive a prize. Everyone eats a piece.

Third cup: Pour and bless the third cup of grape juice.

Inviting Elijah: Pour a cup of grape juice for the prophet Elijah. Open the door and invite Elijah into the home.

Psalms and Prayers: Recite psalms of praise and offer prayers of gratitude.

Fourth cup: Pour the fourth cup of grape juice.

Ending phrase: The text ends with the phrase, "Next year in Jerusalem! Next year may all be free!"

Hymn: Conclude the service with a song.

---

30. Pronounced MA-tzah.
31. Pronounced ma-ROR.
32. Pronounced cha-RO-set.

3
Evolution of the Passover: From Moses to the Present Day

Scholars believe that Passover is "the oldest continuously performed ceremony in the world,"[1] so it is not surprising that the service has changed over the centuries. Tracing the evolution of Passover through the ages reveals a divinely inspired holiday, reinterpreted by every generation, a process that created layers of depth, yet has preserved a central core. The promise of freedom is important to all humanity, but it has special significance for the Jews, who have experienced perilous captivity and miraculous deliverance repeatedly throughout their history. Each generation of Jews receives the words for the Passover Seder from their ancestors, adds their own experiences to it, and passes the new traditions on to their posterity. One rabbi expressed, "The Haggadah mirrors the Jews who composed it. It is not so much recited as experienced. [It provides] an image of our past, a portrait of our present, and a testimony to our faith in the future."[2]

The Time of Moses

The first Passover in Egypt must have been anything but joyous. We can imagine Israelite families huddled in small, dark shacks, forcing themselves to eat the Passover meal, not out of celebration but as sustenance for the long journey

---

1. Steingroot, *op. cit.,* 2.
2. Bronstein and Baskin, *op. cit.,* 12.

41

ahead. They were packed and dressed for travel as they wait-
ed through a long, dark night punctuated with awful screams.
Only one year later, their circumstances were vastly different.
They had walked out of Egypt as a free people, witnessed
Moses part the Red Sea to deliver them from Pharaoh's army,
and received a law from God Himself at the wondrous Mount
Sinai. The escaped slaves of Pharaoh had become "a kingdom
of priests and an holy nation."[3]

Once the Israelites left behind the bondage of Egypt, they
needed new instructions regarding the Lord's will for
Passover observance. After all, Passover was not just a single
occurrence; it was to be "an ordinance forever."[4] The annual
feasts became known as the perpetual Passovers, to differen-
tiate them from the original Passover in Egypt. Leviticus 23,
Numbers 28, and Deuteronomy 16 clarify the Lord's instructions for keeping the perpetual Passover. The Lord declared
that the fourteenth day of the Jewish month Nisan is the official day for Passover observance. Because the Jewish calendar is lunar (as opposed to our solar Gregorian calendar) this
date ensures that every Passover is celebrated on the first full
moon after the Spring Equinox. In addition to sacrificial
lambs, the perpetual Passover was celebrated with grain offerings brought to the tabernacle and Temple sacrifices performed by the priests. On the day after Passover, the Feast of
Unleavened Bread began and for six additional days no leav-
en was eaten. In later years it became difficult to separate
these two festivals, and now the whole seven-day period is
often called Passover.

---

3. Exodus 19:6.
4. Exodus 12:17.

While the Israelites wandered in the desert and conquered the land of Canaan, Passover was observed at various locations. For instance, Joshua's men kept the feast on their way to conquer Jericho.[5] But once the Israelites were firmly established in the Promised Land and the Temple built, the Passover lamb had to be sacrificed on a Temple altar. "At the place which the Lord thy God shall choose . . . there thou shalt sacrifice the Passover at even."[6] Notice that the scripture implies a Temple, but does not specifically mention Jerusalem. In early years, there were many shrines throughout the land of Israel, and people generally observed Passover at the shrine closest to their home. Eventually Jerusalem became the only approved sanctuary, and this commandment in Deuteronomy became extremely significant when the Temple was destroyed centuries later.

The Samaritans

Although the written accounts do not tell us exactly how Passover was celebrated during the early years of Israel's settlement, we gain insight into what it may have been like from the Samaritans, descendants of those left behind when the Assyrians carried off the northern Ten Tribes in 722 B.C. Although the ruling classes were exiled, other conquered peoples were brought in their place. They intermarried with the remaining Israelites, and their descendants later became known as Samaritans.

After the Babylonian exile, the Samaritans attempted to help the Jews rebuild the Temple, but their assistance was refused. The Samaritans set up their own colony on Mount Gerizim in Israel, built another Temple, and continue to cele-

---

5. Joshua 5:10.
6. Deuteronomy 16:6.

brate Passover to this day. After bathing to become ritually
clean, the men are dressed in long, white robes. The lambs are
slain in sacrifice and roasted in large fire pits. Prayers are
recited and psalms are sung. When the food is prepared, the
lambs are lifted out of the pits and families gather together for
the feast. Any leftover food is burned.

Reform under Josiah

Passover was seldom kept during the reign of the kings in
Israel, despite the fact that anyone failing to observe the feast
was to be expelled from the nation.[7] But sadly, after the death
of King Solomon, the Israelites degenerated into dire aposta-
sy. Human sacrifices took place, a house of sodomites stood
beside the house of God, and altars and shrines were built to
Baal and other Canaanite gods inside the holy Temple. Most
kings of Israel encouraged the people's wickedness and
"seduced them to do more evil than did the nations whom the
Lord destroyed before the children of Israel."[8] From this period of six hundred years, there are only two recorded
Passovers. The first occurred under the reign of Hezekiah, a
righteous king who desired to keep the Lord's feast. He invited the children of Israel to repent and gather to Jerusalem,
"for they had not done it [Passover] of a long time."[9] Some of
the Israelites refused to come. They "laughed them to scorn
and mocked them."[10] But others came, and the priests sanctified themselves to perform the Passover sacrifice.

After the reign of Hezekiah, Israel lapsed back into apos-
tasy. In fact, by the time King Josiah came to power, the scrip-

7. Numbers 9:13.
8. 2 Kings 21:9.
9. 2 Chronicles 30:5.
10. 2 Chronicles 30:10.

tures had been lost and forgotten, and Israel had not observed Passover for many years. But at the age of eight, Josiah ruled Israel and he had a profound and permanent effect upon Passover. King Josiah observed that the Temple had fallen into disrepair and decided to have it restored. During the cleaning process, the high priest found the first five books of the Old Testament.

When King Josiah read the forgotten scriptures, he "rent his clothes" and mourned for the nation's wickedness.[11] After consulting the prophetess Huldah, King Josiah gathered "all the people both small and great and he read in their ears all the words of the book of the covenant,"[12] which scholars believe to be the book of Deuteronomy.[13] Then King Josiah stood before them and "made a covenant before the Lord, to walk after the Lord and to keep his commandments . . . with all their heart and all their soul."[14] King Josiah tore down pagan altars, purified the temple, and commanded the people to "keep the Passover as it is written in the book of this covenant."[15] According to 2 Kings, this was the first time Passover had been observed on such a large scale since the reign of the judges began—a span of six hundred years!

In addition to renewing the Passover festival, Josiah permanently changed Israelite worship. Before the days of Josiah, there were local shrines built to Jehovah at Bethel, Samaria, and other locations in Israel. Josiah destroyed every shrine except the Temple in Jerusalem. By making Jerusalem's Temple the only place for Passover observance, the

---

11. 2 Kings 22:11.
12. 2 Kings 23:2.
13. Bandstra, *op. cit.,* 290.
14. 2 Kings 23:3.
15. 2 Kings 23:21.

festival became an occasion for pilgrimage, and the religious focus of the entire nation shifted to Jerusalem. This righteous Israelite King rescued the holy day from neglect and elevated the importance of the Temple as the center of religious observance.

The Freedom Festival in Babylon

Unfortunately, King Josiah's sons were not as righteous as their father, and a few short years after Josiah's death, Israel returned to wickedness. Against the advice of the prophet Jeremiah, the new king of Judah formed an alliance against Babylon, which proved to be a grave mistake. The Lord repeatedly warned the Israelites that if they did not repent, they would be attacked, and in 586 B.C., Babylon conquered Israel. The sacred vessels of the Temple were carried off as war trophies, and Solomon's glorious Temple was defiled and destroyed. The Babylonian army killed many Israelites and carried even more captive to Babylon. As the exiles mourned for their homeland and the Lord's defiled sanctuary, they wrote hymns of sorrow recorded in the book of Psalms. "O God, the heathen are come into thine inheritance; thy holy temple have they defiled; they have laid Jerusalem on heaps."[16]

Fortunately the Babylonians allowed their captives relative freedom once deported, and the Jews made the best of the situation, taking full advantage of opportunities to learn from the Babylonian Empire, one of the most advanced civilizations in the ancient world. The Jews retained Hebrew for religious use, and adopted the Aramaic language, enabling them to access the latest advances in science and technology. Eventually many Jews, including Queen Esther and Daniel,

---

16. Psalms 79:1.

became rich and influential in their new land. It is remarkable that in the midst of this foreign culture, the Jews were able to retain their unique religious identity.

The priests showed an astonishing ability to help the religion adapt to exile. First they began the monumental task of compiling individual scrolls of scripture onto larger scrolls, making them easier to keep track of. Priests combined their scriptural records into three sections the Old Testament still retains today: the Law, the Prophets, and the Writings. Jewish tradition states that Ezra of the Old Testament oversaw this enormous project.

When the five books of Moses were compiled onto a single scroll, the scriptures became centralized, canonized, and accessible. People began to gather into study groups to read and discuss their meaning. The study groups evolved into synagogues, which were houses of study as much as they were places of worship. In these newly formed synagogues, scripture was read to the general public for the first time. Prior to captivity, common people seldom participated in religious ceremonies, but without the Temple, priests recognized that each and every person had to know and understand God's word in order to spiritually survive exile. To understand scripture, a person had to be able to read, so literacy was made a requirement, and soon Jews became the most literate people in the world.

Without the Temple, priests encouraged families to gather and discuss the Exodus on Passover. This counsel shifted the responsibility of Passover away from the public and onto the family community. The festival's promise that God will deliver his people from bondage suddenly gained new relevance for the captives in Babylon. Although the Babylonians allowed them a surprising amount of freedom, the Jews longed to return to Holy Zion. They pleaded with God to rescue them once again from their house of bondage. "By the rivers of Babylon, we sat down and wept when we remembered Zion."[17]

Exiles Return Home

After forty-eight years of bondage, Persia conquered Babylon and the Persian King Cyrus (c. 538 B.C.) decreed that Israelites were allowed to "go up to Jerusalem . . . and build the house of the Lord God of Israel."[18] The children of Israel were free once more. Although some chose to stay in Babylon, many Jews returned to Jerusalem to rebuild the city and the Temple.

The altar was rebuilt first, and priests performed daily sacrifices once again. When they laid the Temple foundation, the children of Israel "sang together by course in praising and giving thanks unto the Lord."[19] The Temple was completed during the reign of King Cyrus' successor, Darius, after twenty years of work. The repaired building was only a shadow of its former glory, but the Temple's rededication was cause for celebration. A meaningful Passover was held as "the priests killed the Passover [lambs] for all the children of the captivity."[20]

Once again, the Israelites had been released from bondage to celebrate their freedom festival. Ezra recorded, "The children of Israel, which were come again out of captivity . . . did eat, and kept the feast of unleavened bread seven days with joy"[21] After seventy long years, God's people were free to fully observe Passover once more.

---

17. Psalms 137:1.
18. Ezra 1:2.
19. Ezra 3:11.
20. Ezra 6:20.
21. Ezra 6:22.

Seder at the Time of Christ

As we have seen, Passover was celebrated prior to the time of Christ, but our knowledge about the actual service is limited. The Bible requires a sacrificial lamb, unleavened bread, bitter herbs, and the teaching of children, but beyond these parameters, no written records exist. As one Jewish scholar records, "The scanty descriptions of the early paschal meal in the later biblical books . . . do not specifically mention any other ceremonial acts. [Therefore] the precise history [of the Seder] must begin toward the end of the Second-Temple period."[22] Fortunately, the Second-Temple period also happens to be the era of Jesus Christ's mortal ministry. Understanding the Seder at this time has much to offer Latter-day Saints.

By the time of Christ, the land of Israel had changed hands once again, and the Jewish nation was under Roman rule. Greco-Roman traditions greatly influenced Israelite culture. Israelites often embraced customs from their rulers, adapting them to fit their own religious traditions. At this time, many aspects of the modern Seder were adopted from a traditional Roman banquet called a symposium.

The Roman symposium was an aristocratic banquet originally created by the Greeks. These banquets consisted of three courses: the hors d'oeuvres usually included eggs, lettuce, or herbs; the main course was often meat or casserole accompanied with sauces and relishes; and a dessert of fruits and nuts finished the banquet. Hands were washed before and after the meal, because food was eaten with fingers instead of utensils.

---

22. Joseph Tabory, "Towards a History of the Paschal Meal," in *Passover and Easter: Origin and History to Modern Times,* eds. Paul F. Bradshaw and Lawrence A. Hoffman (Notre Dame: University of Notre Dame Press, 1999), 5:62-63.

After the meal, the symposium portion began. Participants lounged on cushions surrounding a low table while discussing a prepared topic. It was common to begin the discussion by identifying an ancestor whom all guests had in common to create a sense of unity. Each guest was expected to make a speech on the chosen topic and then offer a toast, which introduced a round of wine drinking. During the symposium, bowls of water and wine were mixed, and a prayer was offered. Usually four wine bowls were mixed, each dedicated to a particular god or ideal (such as hope, life, or love). Discussion topics often included philosophical speculation, recitation of poetry, or the telling of mythical stories. The evening ended with singing hymns to the gods.[23]

Similarities between the Roman symposium and a modern Seder are striking. Many of the same symbolic foods are served, including eggs, parsley, and sauce (charoset). Hands are washed, and four cups of wine are dedicated to particular promises. Identifying the common ancestor Abraham begins the service; participants lounge as they eat; discussion centers on the Exodus; and hymns conclude the ceremony. Apparently the Jews adapted the tradition of their Roman neighbors to create a unique symposium on the topic of the Exodus. Each aspect of the Roman service was infused with Jewish symbolism. Thus, the parsley at the banquet reminded them of the hyssop stalks used anciently to mark doors with lamb's blood; reclining at the table reminded them that they were free; the charoset sauce recalled the brick mortar their

---

23. Blake Leyerle, "Meal Customs in the Greco-Roman World," in *Passover and Easter: Origin and History to Modern Times,* eds. Paul F. Bradshaw and Lawrence A. Hoffman (Notre Dame: University of Notre Dame Press, 1999), 5:29-55.

ancestors made for Pharaoh; and the hymns sung to conclude the service were taken from the psalms the Levites sang at the Temple.

Jewish scholars acknowledge the similarities to the Roman tradition. As one rabbi explained, "There existed a Hellenistic custom of holding sumptuous banquets accompanied by a philosophic conversation. The usual food and practices— such as reclining at the table—were imbued with Jewish symbolic value, and the philosophical discourse was transformed into the Haggadah."[24]

However, definite differences remained between the Jewish Seder and the Roman symposium. For instance, the Roman symposium concluded with after-dinner entertainment and extravagance. Dancing women, gluttonous wine drinking, and flaunted immorality often turned Roman symposiums into raucous parties of debauchery. Of course Jews permitted none of this. The Seder remained a sanctified religious experience, far from associations with worldly pleasures. In place of Roman desserts, Seders conclude by eating a last symbolic bite of unleavened bread, called afikoman, the Greek word for "dessert." The afikoman replaced the after-dinner entertainment, an aspect of the ancient Roman feast that the rabbis eliminated from the Seder so that the entire evening was solely devoted to Passover.

Another difference is the highly elitist nature of the Roman symposium compared with the command for every Israelite family to keep Passover. While only the politically and financially important were included in a symposium, the Jewish people developed a tradition of inviting the stranger, beggar, and the homeless to Seders. This tradition reflected the Jew-

------

24. Bronstein and Baskin, *op. cit.*, 9.

ish teaching that redemption is offered to wealthy and poor alike, and all partake of God's mercy.

Nothing in the Roman symposium could equal the spectacle of Passover sacrifices performed at the Jewish Temple during the life of Christ. Herod the Great rebuilt the Temple for his own political purposes, and the building was truly breathtaking. So impressive was the sight, the Talmud records, "Whoever has not seen Jerusalem in its splendor has never seen a lovely city."[25] Considered one of the wonders of the ancient world, the dazzling Temple rivaled the great Egyptian pyramids for fame. This enormous structure was faced with the whitest marble and adorned with pure gold. Set upon the highest hill in Jerusalem, this towering edifice was the crown of the holy city. In the central court of the Temple, the great altar stood—thirty by thirty feet. Here all of Israel assembled with Passover lambs for sacrificing. Today we can only imagine the sights, sounds, and smells of such a gathering.

Passover lambs were killed in the court of the Temple, then roasted whole and eaten after sunset. One lamb was required for each Israelite family. The law commanded every Jewish male to be present for Passover, so during the month of Nisan, throngs of pilgrims descended upon the city. The usual population of Jerusalem was around thirty to eighty thousand, but it swelled to many times that figure during Passover. Bruce R. McConkie reasoned, "When Nero sat in Caesar's seat a count was made of the number of lambs slain in Jerusalem at one Passover: the total, 256,000. On the basis of a minimum of ten in each group, this meant a Passover population for the holy city of 2,560,000. Josephus placed it that year at 2,700,000 and there were times when the assembled hosts numbered not

_____

25. *Babylonian Talmud,* Succah 51b.

less than 3,000,000."[26] Because all Passover lambs had to be slaughtered in one afternoon, Temple priests developed a remarkable hand-to-hand conveying system in order to provide all of Jerusalem and the pilgrims with sacrificial lambs. The days of Jesus' mortal ministry were truly the height of Passover's glory. Never again would the festival be celebrated with such brilliance and grandeur.

Destruction of the Temple

During his mortal ministry, Jesus prophesied that the Temple would be destroyed. He said, "There shall not be left one stone upon another, that shall not be thrown down."[27] Such a statement must have been difficult to believe at that time, but only forty years after the death and resurrection of Jesus, this prophecy was fulfilled when Roman armies destroyed the Temple and scattered the Jews. The devastating effects of this loss cannot be overestimated. The Temple had been the focus of worship and devotion for the Jewish nation since the days of King Josiah. Without the Temple, it was impossible for the Jews to completely keep the Law of Moses. As Herman Wouk, a Jewish author explained, "The central and most picturesque rite of Passover, the eating of the Paschal lamb, no longer exists. With the fall of the Temple this symbol, like so much of Judaism, went dark."[28]

In the aftermath of this catastrophe, priests struggled to adapt ceremonies so they could be observed without a sanctuary. Although a lamb could no longer be sacrificed, the priests decided the Seder feast could be observed as it had been during the Babylonian exile. Scholars believe that for

---

26. McConkie, *The Mortal Messiah,* 1:163.

27. Mark 13:2.

28. Herman Wouk, *This is My God: The Jewish Way of Life* (New York: Simon and Schuster, 1986), 55.

two generations, "people generally ate a roasted kid . . . and studied the laws of the sacrifice they could no longer perform."[29] Eventually a lamb's shank bone was placed on the Passover table as a reminder of the sacrificial lambs. The bone is called the Zeroah,[30] which means "forearm" in Hebrew. The Zeroah symbolizes the hope and faith of the Jewish people that God's forearm is still extended to His people and some day the Temple will be rebuilt and sacrifices reinstituted.

Centuries after Christ

After the Temple's destruction, rabbis felt the Seder needed more structure to help it survive Judaism's decentralization, so the first Haggadah was created. A rabbi explained, "The original Haggadah was conceived during the tumultuous events of the first century. It was the product of a Jewish generation wrenched from its roots and splintered within its ranks."[31] Although we have documents that discuss the Seder as observed in Jesus' day, the earliest surviving Haggadah is from the Mishnah,[32] a commentary on the five books of Moses, compiled by Rabbi Judah the Prince at the turn of the third century. This Haggadah includes many sections found in modern Haggadahs, including the children's questions, explanations for the symbolic foods, the Exodus story, and specific psalms.

---

29. Israel J. Yuval, "Easter and Passover as Early Christian Dialogue," in *Passover and Easter: Origin and History to Modern Times,* eds. Paul F. Bradshaw and Lawrence A. Hoffman (Notre Dame: University of Notre Dame Press, 1999), 5:114.

30. Pronounced zeh-ro-AH.

31. Bronstein and Baskin, *op. cit.,* 9.

32. Pronounced MISH-nah.

Sometime in the second century, the spoken portion of the service was moved so that it came before the meal. Scholars are not sure why the order was changed, but it may have been a reaction to the adoption of Passover by Jewish Christians in Jerusalem. Gradually, the oral discussion of the Exodus became more fixed in its nature, largely by Rabbi Gamaliel II, the leading sage following the Temple's destruction (c. 120 A.D.). Rabbi Gamaliel taught that the symbolism of the matzah, maror, and charoset should be explained in the service. He also encouraged telling the Exodus story as found in Deuteronomy chapter 26.

At the turn of the third century, a noted leader named Rabbi Tarfon began adding a fifth cup of wine to the Seder service. He taught that this cup was linked to a final, unrealized salvation as expressed in the biblical promise, "I will bring you into the land."[33] Rabbis had always believed ultimate freedom would come on Passover, just as deliverance had occurred on that night so long ago. A Jewish scholar recorded, "For Rabbi Tarfon, the Seder was more than just a lesson in history. It was the making of history, the night of ultimate salvation, God's reentry into history to save Israel again, as He had done so long ago."[34] Rabbi Tarfon's tradition of drinking a fifth cup disappeared for a few centuries, then reappeared, possibly becoming the cup left for Elijah in later years.

Middle Ages

The next recorded version of the Haggadah comes from prayer books dating from c. 860 and 920 A.D. In these renditions, the core of the Haggadah was preserved, while new writ-

---

33. Exodus 6:8.
34. Bronstein and Baskin, *op. cit.,* 11.

ings were added, including philosophical debates of the rabbis. For instance, a third-century section considering whether Israel's bondage was physical or spiritual has been preserved. Most of the precise wording for the Seder was taken from earlier rabbinic writings and the Talmud,[35] a compilation of Rabbinic commentary on the five books of Moses. A section of the Haggadah, called the degradation, which begins, "Our ancestors were slaves in Egypt," was added during this time. Many scholars date the Dayenu poem, which says that each of God's blessings "would have been enough," to the end of the Middle Ages as well, although a persistent few believe it actually dates to the early centuries after Christ.[36]

By the end of the fourteenth century, the medieval Jewish world was reeling from waves of devastation produced by the Crusades, the Inquisition, and pogroms in Europe. This was a terrifying time to be a Jew. Beginning in 613 A.D., Jews in Spain were given the choice between conversion to Christianity and exile. All Jewish children above six years of age were taken from their parents and raised by Christians. When the first of nine Crusades was launched in 1096 A.D., synagogues were burned, Jewish communities were destroyed, and twelve thousand Jews were killed in the Rhine Valley alone. Around 1306 A.D., Jews were expelled from France and England, and one hundred thousand were killed over a six-month period in Austria and Bavaria.

Ironically, periods of Jewish persecution usually reached their climax around Passover. Peaceful holidays were blighted

---

35. Pronounced TAL-mood.

36. Lawrence A. Hoffman, "The Passover Meal in Jewish Tradition." in *Passover and Easter: Origin and History to Modern Times,* eds. Paul F. Bradshaw and Lawrence A. Hoffman (Notre Dame: University of Notre Dame Press, 1999), 5:9.

by false accusations that Jews used the blood of Christian children in making Passover matzah and charoset. This baseless fabrication originated in 1171 A.D. in Blois, France, where the servant of a city official testified that he had witnessed a Jew using a Christian child's blood for ritual purposes. The lie spread across Europe, and the "blood libel" led to the martyrdom of hundreds of thousands of Jews over an eight-hundred-year period in Prague, Vienna, Rome, Bucharest, and Cracow.[37] The accused were usually burned at the stake. Soon, in villages all over Europe, Christians accused Jews of causing almost any misfortune, from outbreaks of the plague to thefts and kidnappings.

As Jews watched their people undergo slaughter in the name of religion, once again they needed God's power to redeem them from bondage. In the midst of their sufferings, they met together for Passover Seders, dreaming of deliverance and revenge. Most of the after-dinner service was created during this period, including additions of poems and songs beseeching the Lord's deliverance, condemning nations that harmed Jews, and affirming faith that God's people would continue to survive against great odds.

In the twelfth century, a great religious fervor swept over Europe, and many felt the Messiah's redemption was imminent. In this climate, the fifth cup of wine reappeared and became known as Elijah's cup. One scholar described, "After reciting a poem (requesting wrath upon one's destroyers), the door was flung open to admit Elijah the prophet, who, it was hoped, would announce the Messiah's imminent arrival."[38] The final line of the service, "Next year in Jerusalem," was

---

37. B.A. Robinson, "2000 Year History of Jewish Persecution," in Ontario Consultants on Religious Tolerance [Database online cited July 14, 2001]; available from http://www.religioustolerance.org.

38. Bradshaw and Hoffman, *Passover and Easter, op. cit.,* 5:20.

added to express the hope that the Messiah would arrive within a year so that the next Passover could be celebrated at the rebuilt Temple in Jerusalem. Although these customs were incorporated into the Seder ceremony at this late date, they simply built on the ancient prophecy that Elijah and the Messiah would arrive at Passover.

Modern Era

The Haggadah text was fluid throughout most of its history, but after the invention of the printing press, textual development was largely frozen for a time. In 1512 the first complete text with illustrations was printed. Soon gorgeously illuminated manuscripts with accompanying songs became popular. By the 1800s, the form was so well known that people protested any attempts at change.

Today, however, most Jews recognize that every generation has reinterpreted the Haggadah's message of freedom in light of their own experiences. A rabbi explained, "Jews at every time and in every place, seeing themselves in the Haggadah's story, have added their own unique contribution to the annual recounting of the miracle of old."[39] For instance, the stories of God releasing his people from bondage gained new applicability for those who lived through the horrors of the Holocaust. Many stories from the concentration camps have been preserved in modern Haggadahs. Today, every Seder is slightly different to fit the experience and needs of each unique family and individual, fitting perfectly with Passover's long history of reinterpretation. As one Jewish scholar wrote, the Haggadah "attempts to relate the past to both the conditions of the present and our hopes for the future."[40]

---

39. Bronstein and Baskin, *op. cit.*, 9.
40. *Ibid.*, 12.

4
Symbols of Christ in Passover

In considering a Christian interpretation of Passover, it is important to be sensitive to the Jewish origins of this holiday. The Book of Mormon criticizes gentiles who believe in the Bible but do not respect the Jews, who compiled and preserved the Bible. It says, "Do they remember the travails, and the labors, and the pains of the Jews, and their diligence unto me, in bringing forth salvation unto the gentiles?"[1] In our eagerness to draw meaning from this holiday, we should not forget to express gratitude for the Jews who recorded its ceremonies and safeguarded them through the centuries. Obviously, Jews do not agree with our interpretation of Passover symbols. They believe the prophecies point to a Messiah yet to come. Above all, we should remember that the service is sacred to others.

It is difficult, if not impossible, to examine all the ways the Passover feast symbolizes the coming of our Savior Jesus Christ. The message of bondage and freedom permeates the entire service, sometimes obviously, while at other times with subtle inferences. To pick apart the symbols and lay them bare would destroy the subtle poetry of the service as a whole. In addition, symbols are complex and shaded with nuance. For instance, a single word in Hebrew often has dozens of possible English equivalents. Prophets who wrote the Hebrew Bible played with this duality of meaning,

---

1. 2 Nephi 29:4.

creating texts filled with a multiplicity of interpretations.
Although we will discuss a few possible interpretations, it is
important to remember that a spectrum of explanations may
be valid. Herman Wouk observed, "If its meaning can be
neatly exposed like the parts of a machine or the solution of a
detective novel, then a symbol lacks the poetry by which
symbols live. But there is nothing wrong with making a par-
tial guess at possible meanings."[2] This chapter only begins to
expound some ways Passover symbolizes Christ. As you and
your family participate in the service, you will discover many
more.

One purpose of Passover is to help every participant personally experience the bitterness of bondage and the sweetness of redemption. Every member of Israel is made aware of
the Lord's mercy in his or her behalf. A Jewish author
explained, "In each generation, Jews experience and reexperience that momentous liberation with the annual celebration
of the Passover holiday. Participating in the Seder—the home
service—each person acknowledges that she/he personally
moved from slavery to freedom."[3] Because every aspect of
the Seder deals with themes of slavery and redemption, the
service can be seen as symbolic of Christ, for he is the one
who makes physical and spiritual freedom possible. Only
through his atoning power may we overcome the bondage of
death and sin.

---

2. Wouk, *This Is My God: The Jewish Way of Life* (New York:
Simon and Schuster, 1986), 57.

3. Karen L. Fox and Phyllis Zimbler Miller, *Seasons for Celebration: A Contemporary Guide to the Joys, Practices, and Traditions of
the Jewish Holidays* (New York: Penguin Putnam, 1992), 117.

Truth Restored

During the Last Supper, the Savior reestablished the link between Passover and the Atonement. He used the traditional Passover symbols of unleavened bread and wine to teach his disciples about his impending sacrifice when he instituted the sacrament. It is crucial to remember that in the LDS perspective, Christ did not change the meaning of the Jewish sacrifices to make them apply to him. The symbolism was there from the beginning. Jesus was the pre-mortal Jehovah who instituted the feast as a shadow and type of his sacrifice, to which he was foreordained from the foundations of the earth. As Jesus explained to Pharisees who rejected him, "Ye keep not the law. If ye had kept the law, ye would have received me, for I am he who gave the law."[4] Clearly, Moses and other prophets understood that the purpose of the Law of Moses was to prepare the people for Christ. Bruce R. McConkie explained, "All things pertaining to his birth and ministry and death and glorification were before taught in the Law of Moses and in the Psalms and in the Prophets."[5]

Therefore, when Christ used Passover emblems to institute the sacrament, he was not giving new meaning to the bread and wine. The symbolism was there all along; he was simply *restoring* original truths lost over the centuries. Members of the restored gospel of Jesus Christ believe we are literally part of the same religion introduced when God first spoke with Adam and commanded him to sacrifice. W. Cleon Skousen said, "Jesus did not initiate Christianity after all. He simply

---

4. JST, Matthew 9:18-20.
5. Bruce R. McConkie, *The Millennial Messiah: The Second Coming of the Son of Man* (Salt Lake City: Deseret Books, 1982), 510.

restored the rich religious culture that God had shared with mankind from the earliest times."[6]

Symbols of the Seder Table

The Seder service is centered on several food symbols. During the course of the evening, these foods are eaten and their symbolism is explained. The tastes are vivid and varied, to rivet the mind on important spiritual truths. For each symbol listed below, first the traditional Jewish interpretation is given, followed by ways in which the symbol may point to Christ. (*Note:* The symbols of Christ are not part of Jewish tradition.)

Candles: White candles on the table serve as symbols of purity and truth, dispelling darkness. They call to mind the light constantly burning in the ancient Temple,[7] a visible reminder of God's enduring truth and prayers of the righteous ascending to heaven. When Passover candles are lit, the mother uses her hand to waft the light toward her face, as if to invite its glow into the home. Light is a recurring symbol of the Savior throughout the scriptures. He is "the light and the life and the truth of the world"[8] and we know that it is by the light of Christ that life on earth is sustained.[9] As darkness cannot fight against light but must flee before it, all evil and wickedness flee before the purity and goodness of the Savior.

Wine or Grape Juice: With its red translucence, the wine (or grape juice) is one of the most vivid symbols on the Passover table. It represents innocent blood shed to buy freedom. The grape juice may call to mind the suffering of the

---

6. Cleon W. Skousen, "The Old Testament Speaks Today," *Ensign,* December 1972, 79.

7. 1 Kings 11:36.

8. Ether 4:12.

9. See *Bible Dictionary,* s.v. "Light of Christ."

children of Israel, or perhaps the innocent Israelite babies slaughtered by Pharaoh. Above all, it symbolizes the blood of the Passover lamb, reverently sacrificed.

Just as blood, a symbol of life itself,[10] was smeared across the doorposts of every Israelite home in Egypt, the blood of our Savior, a pure, undefiled lamb, was also shed to preserve God's children. With sin and death as a consequence of our fallen natures, we are told to "apply the atoning blood of Christ"[11] to the lintels and doors of our hearts, making open confession that we are His. Then his grace is sufficient for us, and we are also passed over, spared by the blood of the Lamb, the "blood which maketh an atonement for the soul."[12] Jesus used Passover wine to institute the sacrament when he told his disciples, "This is my blood . . . which is shed for many for the remission of sins."[13]

Unleavened bread/Matzah: (plural is matzot[14]) Three pieces of unleavened bread are placed on the Seder table. Passover bread is unleavened because yeast is a symbol of oppression. Leavening involves a process of decomposition, as yeast breaks down sugar into carbon dioxide and other by-products. As a symbol of impurity, leaven was not allowed in ancient Temple sacrifices.[15] Thus unleavened bread is "pure" bread. Jewish author Herman Wouk said, "[Yeast] symbolically represents the remnants of the bitter Egyptian slave experience. Jews rid themselves of hametz to reexperience freedom from Egyptian bondage. Leaven is a strange and

10. Leviticus 17:14.
11. Mosiah 4:2.
12. Leviticus 17:11.
13. Matthew 26:28.
14. Pronounced MA-tzot.
15. See Exodus 34:25.

pervasive substance. It is alive; it is immortal; it is impalpably everywhere in the air; it ferments grain into bread, and grapes into wine. No one has ever wholly accounted for this vibrant symbol."[16]

As a symbol of captivity and corruption, leaven is associated with spiritual captivity or sin. The Savior also used this definition when he warned his disciples, "Take heed and beware of the leaven of the Pharisees."[17] In this way, unleavened bread is the perfect symbol of our Savior, the only person who lived a sinless, perfect life. As we prepare ourselves to follow him, so must we try to cast out all leaven/sin in our lives and declare with King Limhi in the Book of Mormon, "O God . . . I will give away all my sins to know Thee."[18]

Bread is used to symbolize the Savior throughout the scriptures. Jesus said, "I am the bread of life, he that cometh to me shall never hunger."[19] In the ancient world, bread was the humblest and most basic of food sources, providing sustenance and nourishment for rich and poor alike. Our Savior said, "Come ye, buy, and eat; yea, come, buy wine and milk without money and without price."[20] He invited all to the feast, sustaining life and nourishing famished souls. As bread has no ability to bless until it is eaten, so also must we take Christ into our lives, allowing his sacrifice to become part of our souls, before we can be healed and converted by his power. The Savior used the matzah as a symbol of his sacrifice when he instituted the sacrament.

---

16. Wouk, *op. cit.,* 59.
17. Matthew 16:6.
18. Alma 22:18.
19. John 6:35.
20. Isaiah 55:1.

Bitter herbs/Maror: The eating of bitter herbs is an essential part of every Seder. Horseradish is most commonly used. After experiencing the bitter sting of raw horseradish during a Passover meal, no one will never forget the poignancy of this appropriately harsh symbol of captivity. We eat the bitter herb to remember the painful lives our ancestors led in captivity. It also reminds us of what existence would be like without a Savior—constrained by sin and the permanence of the grave. The horseradish invites us to imagine the hopelessness of life without assurance of an atoning power. Lacking a Savior, all humanity is captive and bitterness knows no bounds. Alma described this spiritual torture as "racked with eternal torment, for my soul was harrowed up to the greatest degree . . . for which I was tormented with the pains of hell."[21]

Charoset: Charoset is a sauce made from fruit, nuts, and honey. This sticky mixture seems to symbolize a contradiction. On one hand, it recalls the mortar made by the children of Israel in captivity. Yet charoset is also sweet and delicious to the taste. During the Seder, we eat bitter herbs first, then charoset, a stark contrast and a welcome relief. Only after tasting the bitter can we truly appreciate the sweet. Only after we recognize our own inadequacy and captivity can the Savior's atoning power be fully appreciated. As Eve said after the fall, "Were it not for our transgression . . . we never should have known good and evil and the joy of our redemption."[22]

Just as the sweetness of the charoset cannot completely distill the pungent taste of horseradish, so are we never the same after allowing Christ's atonement into our lives. The Haggadah says, "In the time of freedom, there is knowledge

---

21. Alma 36:12.
22. Moses 5:11.

of servitude; And in the time of bondage, the hope of redemption."[23] Although we have been set free, we still remember the darkness we passed through. This helps us to appreciate the light even more. Alma reflected this truth when he recorded, "There could be nothing so exquisite and so bitter as were my pains. Yea, and again . . . on the other hand, there can be nothing so exquisite and sweet as was my joy."[24]

Roasted Egg/Beytzah:[25] Roman banquets were traditionally opened with a hard-boiled egg. The Jews adopted the egg, but roasted it to represent the sacrifices at the ancient Temple, which were burnt upon the altar. When the Jewish Temple was destroyed a few decades after the death of Jesus, it became impossible to fulfill the required Passover sacrifices, so the egg was used as a reminder of sacrifices no longer performed.

The roasted egg also symbolizes life triumphing over death. In the ancient world, eggs were mysterious and wondrous symbols of the circle of life. Eggs appear to be lifeless, but in due time, life appears. Likewise, at a moment when death appeared triumphant, the resurrection brought forth life. Miraculously, Christ was victorious over death, and because of his triumph, all mankind shall live again.

Parsley/Karpas:[26] In some Jewish traditions, parsley represents hyssop branches used by the Israelites to smear lamb's blood on their doorways. The parsley on the Seder table also represents the green growth of springtime when earth awakens from the death of winter and new life begins

---

23. Bronstein and Baskin, *op. cit.,* 9.
24. Alma 36:21.
25. Pronounced bay-TZAH.
26. Pronounced kar-PAS.

again. Similarly, parsley foreshadows the promise of resurrection after the darkness of death. Like the egg, it is a symbol of life's renewal and our Lord's triumph over the grave.

Shankbone/Zeroah:[27] The lamb bone is placed on the Seder plate to remind us of the Passover lamb slaughtered to buy Israelite freedom. Of all the Passover symbols, this is the greatest to Christians, for we believe it foreshadowed the sacrifice of the Lamb of God. John understood this symbol when he wrote, "Behold the Lamb of God which taketh away the sin of the world."[28] Like the Passover lambs, the sinless Son of God was killed to purchase our freedom. "He was wounded for our transgressions, he was bruised for our iniquities: the chastisement of our peace was upon him; and with his stripes we are healed."[29]

Salt water: The tang of salty water in the Seder is sometimes seen as a symbol of the Red Sea which the Israelites passed through on their way to the Promised Land. It brings to mind the tears of those laboring in captivity. The parsley and egg (both symbols of life) are dipped into salt water, creating a symbol of joy and sorrow partaken together. The Seder reminds us that new life was made possible through suffering. We can remember tears the Israelites cried in bondage, but above all, we recall tears the Savior must have shed as he struggled to carry the heavy load of our sins.

Afikoman: On the Passover table, there are three pieces of matzah: two to represent an extra portion of manna the Israelites received on the Sabbath and on holy days, plus an extra piece to be the afikoman. At the beginning of the Seder,

27. Pronounced zeh-ro-AH.
28. John 1:29.
29. Isaiah 53:5.

the middle piece of matzah is broken, wrapped in a napkin, and hidden. Near the end of the Seder, the children search until the afikoman is found. The finder returns it to the table and receives a small prize from the Seder leader. Then everyone eats a piece of the afikoman. This bite of matzah is the last food eaten during the ceremony.

This fascinating tradition is fraught with significance for Latter-day Saints. The three pieces of matzot remind us of the three members of the Godhead. The Godhead consists of the Father, Son, and Holy Ghost: three distinct members united in a single divine will. Christ is the middle member of the Godhead. His body, like the middle matzah, was broken on the cross, wrapped in linen, and hidden away in a tomb. On the third day, light streamed from heaven as the impossible happened: Jesus was resurrected and walked on earth once again. Every Seder participant eats the afikoman, just as every human being who has ever walked on earth will be blessed by the message of the resurrection.

The afikoman may also be seen as a symbol of the Second Coming. Hiding the afikoman represents a world that does not yet recognize Christ as their Lord, "the light which shineth in darkness and the darkness comprehendeth it not."[30] After eating the afikoman, the adults say, "Our hope is in our children to find what is lost, to restore what is broken, to restore our faith." The day will surely come when all hidden truth shall be understood and restored. At the Second Coming, knowledge of the Lord will cover the whole earth and every person who has ever lived will have the opportunity to hear the glad tidings. "At the name of Jesus every knee should bow . . . and every tongue should confess that Jesus Christ is Lord."[31]

30. D&C 6:21.
31. Philippians 2:10-11.

5
Passover in the Life of Jesus

Many events in the Savior's mortal life are best understood when viewed in the context of the Passover festival. As Bruce R. McConkie has said, "Some of his most profound doctrine was taught to the worshipful throngs who assembled to keep the feasts; and miracles, beyond compare, were wrought by his hands at those solemn and sacred times."[1] Knowledge of Passover adds meaning to many of the Savior's teachings and actions. By tracing Passover through Jesus' ministry, we realize that this master teacher used every opportunity to deepen his followers' understanding of prophecies in the Law of Moses he came to fulfill.

In Jesus' day, thousands of Israelites gathered in Jerusalem to celebrate Passover. Josephus speaks of such Passover gatherings as "an innumerable multitude," as people traveled from distant provinces in large companies and caravans.[2] All Jews were expected to present themselves before the Lord at the feast. Each family brought a lamb or goat to sacrifice in the Temple on the eve of the holiday. Then families congregated in the city to roast the lamb over fire. As they ate the lamb with unleavened bread and bitter herbs, they told the story of the Exodus. At the story's conclusion, psalms of praise were chanted.

The Passover feasts of Jesus' day must have been fervent and heartfelt, for Israel was again in bondage. Roman rulers had replaced Greek conquerors, and the Jewish population

---

1. McConkie, *Mortal Messiah,* 1:159.
2. As cited in James E. Talmage, *Jesus the Christ: A Study of the Messiah and His Mission* (Salt Lake City: Deseret Books, 1982), 113.

seethed from the defilement of the Temple decades earlier. Several attempts at Jewish revolt had failed, and a tremulous truce existed between Jewish subjects and their Roman-appointed leaders. Peasant uprisings were common; in fact, one occurred in Galilee just a few years after Christ's birth.[3] The message of the freedom festival must have been particularly poignant in those years. As Jews participated in a service marking their ancestors' deliverance from Egypt, they could not help but consider their own bondage in Palestine.

Teaching in the Temple

Joseph and Mary were devout and faithful in all observances of the law, and "went to Jerusalem every year at the feast of the Passover."[4] Jesus accompanied his parents to the Temple when he was twelve years old, just before his thirteenth birthday, the age at which a Jewish boy was officially accepted as an adult member of the community and, as such, was required to attend the Passover festival in Jerusalem. Most twelve-year-olds "were preparing to become sons of the commandment" in a special bar mitzvah ceremony, where they were allowed to read Scripture before a synagogue congregation for the first time. Jesus probably went with his father to sacrifice the lamb in the Temple and later listened to a family patriarch tell the story of the Exodus.

When festivities concluded, the Galilean caravan traveled a day's journey before Mary and Joseph realized Jesus was not with them. With mounting concern, the worried parents "sought [him] sorrowing"[5] for three long days. Finally they

---

3. Stephen M. Wylen, *The Jews in the Time of Jesus* (New York: Paulist Press, 1996), 75.
4. Luke 2:41.
5. Luke 2:48.

found him "in the Temple, sitting in the midst of the doctors, both hearing them and asking them questions."[6] It was not unusual for a bar mitzvah boy to be questioned by rabbis, for this was part of a Jewish youth's educational training. Nor was there anything surprising about holding such a meeting in the Temple courts, for all ages gathered around the rabbis to learn from their wisdom. But the exchange still astounded the learned doctors, for never before had such a student been found. Indeed, "all that heard him were astonished at his understanding and answers."[7]

We do not know how much Jesus understood about the significance of the sacrifices and his own destiny at this time, nor do we know the topics of discussion that day. But it seems logical that they might have been discussing the Passover feast. As President Howard W. Hunter pondered, "Could it have been possible that Jesus was teaching these older and formally trained men about the meaning of the Passover just celebrated?"[8] Little could the learned men have imagined that the same pre-mortal Jehovah who originally instituted Passover sat among them as a young boy! No wonder they were awed by his comprehension.

Multiplying the Loaves

John recorded that Passover was close at hand when Jesus taught a multitude of five thousand people in the hills of Galilee. As his disciples wondered how they could possibly feed so many, they noticed a young lad with five barley loaves and two fish. Jesus took the boy's offering, blessed it, and

---

6. Luke 2:46.
7. Luke 2:47.
8. Hunter, "Christ, Our Passover," 17.

asked the disciples to distribute it to the hungry crowd. When everyone had eaten, twelve baskets of food remained.

Why did John make a point of telling us that this occurred at Passover time? When the crowd saw the miracle Jesus had performed, they said, "This is of a truth that prophet that should come into the world."[9] Centuries earlier, when the children of Israel were hungering in the wilderness, Moses miraculously provided manna, or "bread from heaven."[10] Prophecies held that although manna had ceased with Moses, it would return with the Messiah, and the Messiah was expected to return at Passover time. Thus, when Jesus miraculously fed thousands in the Galilean hills, it was a miracle much like Moses', and the action carried profound significance for his listeners.

The next day, when the same multitude followed Jesus again, he continued to teach them about the implications of this miracle. "Your fathers did eat manna in the wilderness and are dead. I am the living bread which came down from heaven: if any man eat of this bread, he shall live forever: and the bread that I will give is my flesh, which I will give for the life of the world."[11] His listeners were shocked that Jesus proclaimed himself to be the fulfillment of a Messianic prophecy—living manna sent by God. The skeptical crowds murmured, "Is not this Jesus, the son of Joseph, whose father and mother we know?"[12] Although they knew his mortal mother Mary, they did not comprehend that Joseph was but an earthly guardian, for his father was God Himself.

---

9. John 6:13-14.
10. John 6:31.
11. John 6:49, 51.
12. John 6:42.

When Jesus presented the doctrine of eating his flesh and drinking his blood it was a profoundly disturbing doctrine for his audience. To us today, this principle makes sense because we partake of the symbols of his sacrifice in the sacrament. But to his original listeners, the cannibalistic image reminded them of the pagan rituals of their Canaanite neighbors. The children of Israel had been commanded to shun human sacrifice, although at the height of their wickedness (586 B.C.), many adopted the heinous practice. The Lord's wrath was unleashed upon those who "mingled among the heathen and shed innocent blood . . . who sacrificed unto the idols of Canaan and the land was polluted with blood."[13]

When Jesus spoke of eating his flesh and blood, it is not surprising that many of the disciples said, "This is a hard saying; who can hear it?"[14] From that time, many of his followers turned away and "walked no more with him."[15] Only the spiritually attuned could understand Jesus' teaching. For those willing to see, Jesus showed that he had come to fulfill the prophecies of Moses. He was "the true bread from heaven . . . which cometh down from heaven and giveth life unto the world." [16] Later, the disciples learned that the symbol of eating bread foreshadowed the institution of the sacrament and illustrated the life-giving power of the Atonement.

Feeding bread to thousands in the wilderness and teaching a discourse on the "bread of life" were perfectly timed. In a few days, his listeners would be observing the Feast of Unleavened Bread and recounting the miracles of Moses. Introducing this principle immediately before Passover gave

---

13. Psalms 106:35-38.
14. John 6:60.
15. John 6:66.
16. John 6:33

his listeners the opportunity to ponder his words as they partook of ancient symbols.

Cleansing the Temple

In the first year of his public ministry, Jesus went up to Jerusalem for the Passover feast. When he saw moneychangers and those selling animals for sacrifices within the temple walls, he overthrew their tables and drove them out with a whip. Three years later, he repeated the cleansing of the Temple when he went to Jerusalem for his last Passover feast, days before his death. It is remarkable the Savior chose to cleanse the Temple shortly before the first and last Passovers of his public ministry. Symbolically, Jesus' actions recall the Jewish tradition of ridding the home from all leaven and sin in preparation for the Passover feast. By assuming responsibility to purify the Temple for Passover, he declared that the Temple was his home.

Anointed One

Mary, the sister of Lazarus, came before Jesus and his disciples one week before Passover as they sat at meat. She brought an alabaster box of costly ointment and anointed Jesus' head and feet. Everything we know about Mary suggests great spiritual sensitivity. It seems that she understood, perhaps even more than the disciples, the events that would soon take place. When a disciple complained the ointment could have been given to the poor, Jesus explained, "she did it for my burial."[17]

In ancient Israel, prophets, high priests, and kings were consecrated and set apart to their offices in an anointing ceremony. The Hebrew word "Messiah" literally means

---

17. Matthew 26:12.

"anointed one." The rabbinical tradition taught the faithful to expect the Messiah to return at Passover time, and indeed Passover reminded Israel that, as God had delivered His people in the past, so He would deliver them again through the Messiah. One must suppose that Mary had this meaning in mind when she performed this beautiful act. Earlier, Mary's sister testified, "I believe that thou art the Christ, the Son of God, which should come into the world."[18] By anointing Jesus publicly, Mary also testified openly and unmistakably that he was the promised Messiah—her Prophet, Priest, and King.

Strife Among the Apostles

The gospels give slightly varying accounts of the Last Supper of Christ. According to Luke 22, Matt 26, and Mark 14, the last supper was a Passover Seder. Mark records that after killing the Passover lamb in the Temple, his disciples asked Jesus where they would eat the Seder. He told them they would find a man who would take them to a large upper room. "And his disciples went forth, and came into the city, and found as he had said unto them: and they made ready the Passover."[19] After the disciples prepared the room for the Seder, the Savior joined them.

As they sat down to the meal, strife arose concerning who was the greatest among the disciples. The seats at Roman symposia were precisely arranged to reflect the hierarchy of guests. A scholar explained, "The couches themselves were carefully ranked so that one could tell at a glance who was the most honored guest—and who the least."[20] This custom

---

18. John 11:27.
19. Mark 14:16.
20. Blake Leyerle, *Passover and Easter, op. cit.,* 5:31.

suggests a possible reason contention arose. However, Jesus taught them that status in the world has no place in the kingdom of God: "Ye know that the princes of the Gentiles exercise dominion over them and they that are great exercise authority upon them. But it shall not be so among you; but whosoever will be great among you, let him be your minister and whosoever will be chief among you, let him be your servant."[21] At his last Seder, Jesus showed it is more important to be great in the eyes of God than to receive the praise of man.

The Last Seder

As Jesus and his disciples shared their last Seder meal, the disciples expected the ceremony to follow customs they were well familiar with. They had grown up with these traditions, and must have spent other Seders with Jesus. But this night held wondrous surprises for them. The first shock came as the party dipped bitter herbs and matzah into the charoseth sauce, served in a communal bowl. As they did so, Jesus revealed that one of the disciples who "dippeth with me in the dish" would betray him.[22] John records that Judas left shortly thereafter to perform the evil deed, leaving Jesus alone with the faithful eleven.

As the meal commenced, Jesus gave another indication that this would be no ordinary Seder. He said, "With desire have I desired to eat this Passover with you before I suffer."[23] Observing Passover shortly before his suffering gave the Savior the opportunity to teach and prepare his disciples for what lay ahead.

---

21. Luke 22:25-27.
22. Mark 14:20.
23. Luke 22:15.

The Seder traditionally began with the prayer known as the kiddush,[24] or "sanctification of the day." This prayer was recited over the first cup of wine. Luke implies that Jesus said this prayer when he recorded, "He took the cup and gave thanks."[25] Although the words are not recorded in the scriptures, part of the customary prayer was "Blessed art Thou, Oh Lord, our God, who sanctifies this day and brings forth fruit from the vine." Then Jesus took the unleavened bread, blessed it, and broke it according to custom. The traditional prayer was "Blessed art Thou, Oh Lord, our God, who sanctifies this day and brings forth bread from the earth." So far, the rituals had been performed according to the disciples' expectations.

As the Matzah was passed around, it was time for Jesus, as leader of the Seder, to explain the meaning of the unleavened bread. The disciples expected him to say, "This is the bread of affliction which our ancestors ate in the wilderness," and proceed with the story of the Exodus. Instead, he instructed them, "This is my body which is given for you. This do in remembrance of me."[26]

Because we are familiar with this story, it does not have the same thunderbolt effect that it would have had for the apostles. Their reaction must have been instantaneous: *What did Jesus say? What could he mean?* This ceremony was a sacred, holy part of their religion. A modern equivalent would be our own reaction to someone who suddenly changed the words of the sacrament prayer! The scriptures do not record the disciples' shock, nor the Savior's patient explanations. Perhaps he gently clarified that he alone had the right to reveal the true meaning of the Passover symbols, since he had

---

24. Pronounced KID-oosh.
25. Luke 22:17.
26. Luke 22:19.

revealed them in the first place as the pre-mortal Jehovah. Finally, after centuries of time, the symbols of the Seder were again described with the full truth that Moses understood when Jehovah instituted them through his prophet. The Savior thus prepared his disciples to witness the fulfillment of the Law of Moses only a few short hours later.

From the scriptural account, it appears the Seder progressed for a time according to tradition. Four cups of wine were poured and blessed. Like all Jews, the disciples knew that four cups of wine had been added to the feast to symbolize the four ways that God promised to redeem his people in the book of Exodus. The first promise is "I will bring you out from under the burdens of the Egyptians." The second is "I will deliver you from their bondage." The third is "I will redeem you with an outstretched arm." And the fourth is "I will take you to me for a people and I will be to you a God and ye shall know that I am the LORD your God, which bringeth you out from under the burdens of the Egyptians."[27]

Luke recorded that "When it was time for the "cup after supper"[28] Jesus again gave thanks, probably using the usual blessing, "Blessed art Thou, oh Lord, our God, Master of the universe, who brings forth fruit from the vine." But instead of the discussion on spiritual bondage the disciples expected, Jesus held up the cup and explained, "Drink ye all of it; for this is my blood of the new testament, which is shed for many for the remission of sins."[29] Again, shock must have filled the room as the disciples realized the Savior was using the "passover wine" as a symbol of his sacrifice.

Most scholars believe that Jesus used the third cup of the Passover to institute the Sacrament, but others feel that the

27. Exodus 6:6-7.
28. Luke 22:20.
29. Matthew 26:27-28.

fourth cup may have been more likely. Whether the Savior used the third cup or the fourth, the symbolism remains appropriate. The promise for the third cup is that of redemption. (For the meaning of the title "redeemer," see page 89).

But if indeed the Savior used the fourth cup to institute the sacrament, the choice of this symbol could not be more perfect. The two-way nature of the fourth cup's promise, "You will be my people, and I will be your God," implies a covenant relationship between God and his children. Because of the Savior's sacrifice, he can claim us as his own; and we, in turn, take his name upon us. He becomes our "advocate with the Father, who is pleading your cause before him, saying, 'Father, behold the sufferings and death of him who did no sin . . . wherefore, Father, spare these my brethren that believe on my name.'"[30] Truly, it is the cup of the Atonement that allows us to become one of His children.

The second part of the promise of the fourth cup of wine is equally important. It says, "Ye shall know that I am the LORD your God." The word LORD in the Old Testament is actually the sacred name of God we translate today as Jehovah. In the ancient world, this holy name was never spoken, in order to show utmost reverence. Instead, the holy name was read as "Adonai," which means "Lord." But the word "Lord" is also the title given to earthly leaders or masters. To separate the common word from the deferential title given to God Himself, the King James translators identified the name of deity by using all capital letters: LORD. Therefore, another valid translation of the scriptural promise reads, "Ye shall know that I am JEHOVAH, your God, which bringeth you out from under the burdens of the Egyptians."

---

30. D&C 45:3-5.

This scripture promises the children of Israel that they will know and recognize their God and deliverer. Surely the agony of the Atonement identified the Savior as the promised Messiah, separate and unique from all other great spiritual leaders. Only a God could have survived the suffering in Gethsemane and stay in mortality; only a God had power to lay down His life and take it up again on the third day. Jesus performed the infinite sacrifice, showing that he alone had the power to bring freedom from death and sin. He fulfilled Isaiah's prophecy: "Therefore my people shall know my name: therefore they shall know in that day that I am he that doth speak: behold it is I."[31]

After drinking the last cup of the Seder, Jesus and his disciples "sang a hymn," according to Jewish custom.[32] The hymn was probably from the book of Psalms, which served as Israel's hymnbook in the Temple. Today it is customary to recite extracts from Psalms 115-118, but in Jesus' time there were several Psalms that might have been chosen. At that momentous Passover, it seems likely that one of the Messianic Psalms would have been selected. This passage from Psalms 116 is still said at Passover: "O LORD, truly I am thy servant; I am thy servant, and the son of thine handmaid: thou hast loosed my bonds."[33]

Passover and the Sacrament

Although the disciples did not realize it until later, the Savior used the Seder service as his last lesson to them. He tried to prepare them as much as possible for the events, both sacred and terrifying, that followed. Only later did they understand how Jesus had selflessly served them, even until the end. He

---

31. Isaiah 52:6.
32. Mark 14:26.
33. Psalms 116:16.

devoted the last few moments before his suffering to leaving them with a covenant of protection and peace—the sacrament.

To truly understand this, we must remember Jesus knew the Mosaic Law would be fulfilled after his death. Blood sacrifices would no longer be effective, and saints would be left without an ordinance enabling repentance and reconciliation with God. The word sacrifice means "to make holy,"[34] and indeed that is what ancient sacrifices did. They acted as purification ceremonies between God and his people (see Leviticus 4:20). They were performed as symbols of the ultimate sacrifice of our Savior, whose sacrifice sanctifies all who come unto him. As the Apostle Paul explained, the law of Moses was "our schoolmaster to bring us unto Christ,"[35] providing "a shadow of good things to come."[36]

Knowing that the time of fulfillment was at hand, Jesus didn't want to leave the disciples without comfort and protection; so he instituted the sacrament to provide a link between sacrifices foreshadowing the Atonement and his final sacrifice fulfilling the law. Instead of looking forward, believers would now remember the past. The word sacrament means "to remember that which made us holy."[37] Instead of anticipating a future redemption, saints now meet in remembrance of that "which made us holy." As Bruce R. McConkie wrote, "Our Lord instituted the ordinance of the sacrament to serve

---

34. *Webster's Ninth New Collegiate Dictionary.* s.v. "sacrifice," Prefix sacr- in Latin, meaning "sacred" and suffix -fice from French *facere* which means "to make."

35. Galatians 3:24.

36. Hebrews 10:1.

37. *Webster's Ninth New Collegiate Dictionary.* s.v. prefix "sacr," in Latin, meaning "sacred" and s.v. suffix "ment," meaning "concrete result" in Latin.

essentially the same purposes served by the sacrifices of the preceding four millenniums."[38]

The connection between sacrifice and sacrament remains an important one. In modern-day revelation, the Lord commands us to "offer up thy sacraments upon my holy day."[39] The phrase "offer up" recalls the altars in the ancient Temple where blood sacrifices were performed. Even today the sacrament is prepared on an altar, reminding us that sacrifice is an eternal law. We come before the sacrament altar to "offer up" our sacrifice—our sins, our commitment, our will, a broken heart, and a contrite spirit.[40]

Passover helped the Israelites experience, first, the bitterness of bondage and then the sweetness of release. This is also the purpose of the sacrament. President Howard W. Hunter taught that as the Passover was a covenant of protection for ancient Israel, the sacrament is a "new covenant of safety" for us.[41] It is a time to remember our sins, sincerely repent with sorrow, and take the emblems in remembrance of Christ's gift. When sincerely partaken of, the sacrament allows the spirit of God to flow into our newly cleansed hearts as we promise to "always remember him."[42] Through the sacrament, we feel a renewal of gratitude for he who made deliverance possible. We personally recognize Jesus as our Messiah, Savior, and Redeemer. There is immense power to be found in the sacrament. As Elder Jeffrey R. Holland asked,

---

38. Bruce R. McConkie, *The Promised Messiah: The First Coming of Christ* (Salt Lake City: Deseret Book Co., 1978), 426.
39. D&C 59:9.
40. D&C 97:8.
41. Howard W. Hunter, "His Final Hours," *Ensign,* May 1974, 18.
42. D&C 20:77.

"Do we see [the sacrament] as *our* Passover, remembrance of *our* safety and deliverance and redemption?"[43]

Washing the Apostles' Feet

While the synoptic gospels highlight the institution of the sacrament, John's account recorded Jesus' teachings after the meal. When Jesus knelt and washed the feet of the disciples, he did so within the context of a tradition. At a Roman symposium, the host's slaves often wound garlands around the guest's ankles or anointed their feet. But in this instance, it was the master who performed the menial service. This is why Peter was so horrified when the Savior approached to cleanse him. He exclaimed, "Thou shalt never wash my feet."[44] Gently, Jesus taught his disciple, "Ye call me Master and Lord and ye say well; for so I am. If I then, your Lord and Master, have washed your feet; ye also ought to wash one another's feet. For I have given you an example, that ye should do as I have done to you."[45] What a significant contrast his actions provide to the strife over seating arrangements before the supper began! Once again the Savior demonstrated kindness and humility.

As he ministered to them, Jesus spoke to the disciples about peace, the necessity of his death, and the Holy Ghost. He prayed for his followers and gave them a new commandment to love one another. This poignant discussion seems to have replaced the usual Passover after-dinner discussion. Perhaps John's account may be thought of as the surviving Haggadah from that very special Seder.

---

43. Jeffrey R. Holland, "This Do in Remembrance of Me," *Ensign*, November 1995, 68.

44. John 13:8.

45. John 13:8, 13-15.

Atonement: The Bitter Cup

Immediately following the Seder, Jesus led his disciples out of Jerusalem's gates, down through the Kidron valley, and up to the Mount of Olives. Somewhere on this mountain (we do not know the exact location today) was a place called Gethsemane. There the Savior continued the symbolism of the passover cup of wine when he prayed, "Father, if thou be willing, remove this cup from me: nevertheless, not my will, but thine be done."[46] Centuries of prophecy, indeed every communication between God and man, had looked forward to this event as the culmination of the sacrificial ordinances. The Savior was willing to drink the bitter atoning cup, allowing us to become his people. As he suffered, he sweat drops of blood from every pore—red liquid so similar to the wine chosen to symbolize his sacrifice.

No mortal can atone for the sins of another,[47] nor could any mortal man have endured what Christ did and live. Only the fact that his physical body was partly divine, as inherited from his Eternal Father, gave him the strength to suffer the pain he experienced and not perish. James E. Talmage wrote of this moment, "Christ's agony in the garden is unfathomable by the finite mind, both as to intensity and cause. He struggled and groaned under a burden such as no other being who has lived on earth might even conceive as possible. It was not physical pain, nor mental anguish alone, that caused Him to suffer such torture as to produce an extrusion of blood from every pore; but a spiritual agony of soul such as only God was capable of experiencing."[48]

---

46. Luke 22:42.
47. Alma 34:10-14.
48. Talmage, *op. cit.*, 568.

It was late at night when the Creator of the world knelt all alone in a garden. There he took upon himself all the burdens, sins, and sorrows of the human race. His empathy was perfected through composite suffering. These moments in Gethsemane could be called the spiritual climax of all human history, and yet deliverance came so quietly that even his disciples could not keep from sleeping through the experience. Was this hour of freedom arbitrarily chosen? Was it mere coincidence that this night of atonement occurred shortly after the Savior participated in the Seder? For it was also on the eve of Passover, "about midnight," when the spirit of the LORD swept through Egypt, slaying the first-born of the Egyptians, while sparing the Israelite homes marked with blood![49] The symbol and its fulfillment occurred at the same day and time, bridging the centuries.

The timing chosen for the world's spiritual deliverance remarkably fulfills a Jewish tradition. Rabbis had assumed all along that Passover Eve was the time scheduled for the ultimate redemption and return of the Messiah. One rabbi explained, "Legend had it that just as deliverance had occurred on this night so long ago, so ultimate freedom would again come about on Passover."[50] The tradition of opening the door for Elijah is linked to this prophecy and dates to Temple times. The historian Josephus records that priests opened the Temple doors shortly after midnight on Passover. The doors were opened to invite and welcome redemption, which was expected at that hour. Even today the afikoman must be eaten by midnight and the doors are opened for Elijah shortly thereafter. Rabbi Joshua taught, "On that night they were redeemed in the past and on that night they will be redeemed in the

49. Exodus 11:4.
50. Bronstein and Baskin, *op. cit.,* 11.

future."[51] Truly these traditions were correct, for redemption did occur on Passover Eve—in a garden called Gethsemane.

Crucifixion: The Blood of a Lamb

Several events leading to Jesus' crucifixion are connected to Passover. When Jesus was taken to Caiaphas' palace, the Jewish leaders refused to enter the Roman hall, believing that their entry there would make them unworthy to eat the Passover meal. Pilate was requested to hear their complaint outside. John recorded, "They themselves went not into the judgment hall, lest they should be defiled, that they might eat the Passover."[52] These leaders once more looked beyond the mark as they worried primarily about their own ritual purity, believing that they could unjustly condemn a guiltless man and yet remain worthy to eat a sacred meal.

When Pilate tried to spare Jesus, the Passover festival was mentioned again. There was a Jewish custom of releasing a prisoner at Passover time, an appropriate tradition for the "freedom festival." Hoping to save Jesus, Pilate offered to save the innocent prisoner, but an angry crowd chose instead to free Barrabbas, a robber and murderer.[53] Thus they chose to trade the existence of one who brought life for one who robbed life. But in reality, the decision was never theirs to make. Jesus, the Son of God, could not be held against his will. He said, "Thinkest thou that I cannot now pray to my Father, and he shall presently give me more than twelve legions of angels?"[54] Our Savior humbly allowed himself to

51. Hoffman, *op. cit.,* 5:20.
52. John 18:28.
53. John 18:39.
54. Matthew 26:53.

be bound in order to bring freedom into the world—even to those who sat in judgment against him.

Precise timelines for the events in Gethsemane and Calvary vary in the gospel accounts. The synoptic gospel writers place Gethsemane's anguish late at night on Passover Eve and the crucifixion on the following day. The gospel of John, however, describes the last supper as an ordinary meal, not a Seder.[55] In John's account, Jesus was crucified on the Eve of Passover, a one-day discrepancy. John recorded that Jesus died in the sixth hour, at mid-afternoon—at exactly the same time the Passover lambs were sacrificed in the Temple. Various theories reconciling these discrepancies exist.[56] One belief is that the increasingly large number of lambs to be slain necessitated that the sacrifices be performed on two consecutive days.

We can see this discrepancy as merely an historical dilemma, or we can view it as representative of two different views of religious emphasis. Both versions add meaning to our knowledge of the Atonement. In the synoptic gospels, emphasis is on Gethsemane as the moment of redemption, with the sacrament emblems as the crucial elements. In John's account, Christ's suffering on the cross is the climax of the Atonement, the paschal lamb the most important symbol. This debate continues today as some Christian groups emphasize the suffering on the cross, while others focus on the prayer in Gethsemane. LDS theology reconciles these views by teaching that Jesus suffered the effects of sin in the garden and of death upon the cross.

---

55. John 19:14.
56. For a broader review of these theories, see Talmage, 617-19.

As a witness of Jesus' fulfillment of the Passover sacrifice, John recorded several ties between the crucifixion and Passover symbols. For instance, when he wrote, "Behold the Lamb of God, which taketh away the sin of the world,"[57] he assumed that his readers would understand the significance of sacrificial lambs in the Passover ceremonies. Rules for choosing Passover lambs were exacting and stringent. They had to be males of the first year, and without blemish. No bone could be broken when they were slaughtered. The lambs had to be perfect—worthy symbols of the spotless One who would come to save.

The intact bones of Passover lambs foreshadowed the death of the Savior. As part of the Roman crucifixion process, it was common practice to hasten the victim's death by breaking his legs. Thieves, crucified on either side of the Savior, had their legs broken. Yet when they came to Jesus, he had already died, so his bones remained intact. Instead, a spear was thrust into his side, fulfilling prophecy.[58]

Another Passover symbol was present during the crucifixion, when vinegar was offered to Jesus on a branch of hyssop.[59] On the night of the first Passover, the Israelites used hyssop to apply lamb's blood to their doorposts. The link between hyssop and purification is made by the psalmist when he wrote, "Purge me with hyssop and I shall be clean; wash me, and I shall be whiter than snow."[60] It was fitting for hyssop to be present when the Savior purified the world through his suffering.

---

57. John 1:29.
58. John 19:31-36.
59. John 19:29.
60. Psalms 51:7.

The pain Jesus experienced upon the cross must have been excruciating—beyond the greatest reaches of our imagination. What a debt of gratitude we owe to he who bought us freedom. "Were it not for the redemption which he hath made for his people . . . all mankind must have perished."[61]

Redeemer of the World

The commonly used title "redeemer" is tied to Passover. In the ancient world, if a man owed a debt he could not pay, he would be sold into slavery to pay the bond. Thus, stripped of the ability to earn the money to buy his freedom, he was doomed to a life of slavery. If a third party chose to pay the debt, the slave then belonged to this new master; however, such a person had the option of willingly freeing the prisoner. One who performed this charity was called a "redeemer."

What a fitting title for Jesus Christ, who saw us hopelessly in bondage and willingly paid the awful price to carry our sins. He paid our debts, and technically we now belong to him as the following scripture reflects: "What? Know ye not that . . . ye are not your own? For ye are bought with a price."[62] Yet he is a merciful Savior, who prizes our free agency above all. He paid the price for everyone, whether they accept deliverance or not. Then he set us free, becoming a true redeemer.

The great message of Passover is that all enslaved are invited to come unto the One with power "to bind up the brokenhearted, to proclaim liberty to the captives, and the opening of the prison to them that are bound."[63] As our ancestors were redeemed when they were bought out of slavery, so are we.

---

61. Mosiah 15:19.
62. 1 Corinthians 6:20.
63. Isaiah 61:1.

Resurrection Morning: The Captives Shall Go Free

Before Easter morning, death represented a bitter, inescapable bondage. Modern-day revelation helps us understand this principle. In the Doctrine and Covenants, we learn that "spirit and element, inseparably connected, receive a fullness of joy. And when separated, man cannot receive a fullness of joy."[64] We glimpse the joy of resurrection in President Joseph F. Smith's Vision of the Redemption of the Dead. He saw a great multitude of spirits who had lived righteously during mortality, including Adam and Eve and prophets such as Elijah, Abraham, and Isaiah. These spirits gathered together, awaiting the arrival of Christ and their subsequent resurrection. "For the dead had looked upon the long absence of their spirits from their bodies as bondage."[65] When Christ arrived, they received him with delight. "And the saints rejoiced in their redemption, and bowed the knee and acknowledged the Son of God as their Redeemer and Deliverer from death and the chains of hell."[66]

When Jesus arose from the tomb on that Sunday morning, he broke the bands of death for every person who has, or ever will, come into the world. Until that point, no one had ever returned from beyond the grave. We can imagine the glorious thrill of that day when graves of righteous saints were opened and people saw loved ones long deceased. The promise of the resurrection is that because the Savior lived again, so shall we. With the dawning of resurrection morning, Passover prophecies were fulfilled. Jesus had overcome the bondage of both sin and death—the two great plagues of humanity lay

---

64. D&C 93:33-34.
65. D&C 138:50.
66. D&C 138:23.

conquered. Truly, Jesus snatched us from the bands of bondage and brought us to rejoice in the brilliant light of God's freedom. Because of him, we are "delivered from the bondage of corruption into the glorious liberty of the children of God."[67] As one Passover song declares:

> Therefore, let us rejoice
> At the wonder of our deliverance
> From bondage to freedom
> From agony to joy,
> From mourning to festivity,
> From darkness to light,
> Before God let us ever sing a new song.[68]

Development of Easter

After the resurrection of Jesus, the early Christian saints continued to celebrate Passover according to Jewish traditions, but as they celebrated the feast, they honored symbolism pointing to Christ. A scholar explained, "The celebration of Pascha (as Easter was known) began life as the Christian version of Passover, observed on the same day as its Jewish antecedent and focused upon Christ as the paschal lamb who had been sacrificed for the sins of the world."[69] These early Jewish Christians testified that Jesus was the Passover lamb, slain for all. They met to affirm that like the broken matzah, Jesus allowed his body to be broken, and, above all, to testify

---

67. Romans 8:2.
68. Bronstein and Baskin, *op. cit.,* 57.
69. Paul F. Bradshaw, "Easter in Christian Tradition," in *Passover and Easter: Origin and History to Modern Times,* eds. Paul F. Bradshaw and Lawrence A. Hoffman (Notre Dame: University of Notre Dame Press, 1999), 5:1.

that the sacrifice of the Savior brought freedom for their ancestors as well as to their posterity.

Clearly, a Christian celebration of Passover is not without precedent; in fact, it has been part of Christianity since the earliest times. Some scholars believe that Mark's Gospel was written right after the Temple's destruction, as a Christian-Jewish Haggadah for Passover.[70] Paul was referring to the tradition of Pascha when he wrote, "Christ our Passover is sacrificed for us. Therefore let us keep the feast . . . with the unleavened bread of sincerity and truth."[71]

The day we now observe as Easter was established at the Council of Nicea, in 325 A.D. when arguments to lessen the Jewish influence on Easter prevailed. The Council of Nicea's anti-Semitic sentiments were expressed in statements such as, "It is unbecoming beyond measure that on this holiest of festivals we should follow the customs of the Jews. Henceforth let us have nothing in common with this odious people."[72] By the fourth century, Pascha was transferred to Sunday to honor the day of the Resurrection. An LDS author explained, "This decision involved rejecting the Jewish calendar system in favor of the Julian calendar system when identifying the date for Easter. The Resurrection occurred 'on the first day of the week' (Luke 24:1), and since Sunday is the first day of the Julian week, Sunday was selected for Easter celebration."[73]

The holiday gradually moved further and further away from its Jewish roots, eventually adopting the name of the

---

70. Israel J. Yuval, *Passover and Easter, op. cit.*
71. 1 Corinthians 5:7-8.
72. David Rosenthal, "Blighted Passover Days and Blood Libels," in *Jewish Frontier: A Labor Zionist Journal,* [Database online cited Jan-Aug 2000]; Available from http://www.jewishfrontier.org.
73. Robert C. Patch, "I Have a Question," *Ensign,* April 1982, 29.

Norse goddess, Eastre, whose festival was observed at the vernal equinox. The egg eaten at the Passover Seder was transformed into the Easter egg. Traditional pagan symbols of spring, such as bunnies and flowers, were added to the holiday over several centuries.

6
Passover and Latter-day Prophecy
Passover in the Book of Mormon

Passover is never specifically mentioned in the Book of Mormon, although it was surely observed as part of the Mosaic Law, which the Nephites had recorded on the plates of brass. Passover on the American continent would have been celebrated as a symbol of Christ, for Nephite prophets reminded the people that the law was a herald of good things to come. Nephi wrote, "Behold, my soul delighteth in proving unto my people the truth of the coming of Christ; for, for this end hath the law of Moses been given; and all things which have been given of God from the beginning of the world, unto man, are the typifying of him."[1]

Although the Book of Mormon does not specifically identify any Passovers, there are a few instances that may be Passover-related. For instance, when King Benjamin invites his people to gather at the Temple and hear his words, they gather with "the firstlings of their flocks, that they might offer sacrifice and burnt offerings according to the law of Moses."[2] This gathering at the Temple to perform sacrifices might have been during any of the pilgrimage festivals, but there are a few hints that link it with Passover. First, the Nephites came "to give thanks to the Lord their God, who had brought them out of the land of Jerusalem, and who had delivered them out of the hands of their enemies."[3] This goal for the gathering is

---

1. 2 Nephi 11:4.
2. Mosiah 2:3.
3. Mosiah 2:4. Other LDS authors have suggested that this may have been during the Feast of the Tabernacles. See "Recent Studies on the Book of Mormon," *Ensign,* June 1989, 50.

in harmony with the celebration of Passover. It is interesting to consider the similarity between the deliverance of the Israelites from Egypt and the deliverance of Lehi's family from Jerusalem. Certainly, during Nephite Passovers, Lehi's journey across the ocean would have been seen as a continuation of the Passover epic.

The second hint that may tie King Benjamin's discourse to Passover occurs at the end of his speech, when the people collectively make a covenant to keep the words of the Lord as explained by King Benjamin. This experience is remarkably similar to the council King Josiah held during a Passover celebration as recorded in 2 Kings 23. In both situations, the people are called together to the Temple, the King reads scripture and admonishes, and the people make a covenant with the Lord to follow Him. Perhaps the story of King Josiah, recorded on the plates of brass, was a model for King Benjamin's gathering.

Another portion of the Book of Mormon that may be related to the observance of Passover is best understood in context of the following scripture: "And thou shalt tell thy son in that day, saying, This [Passover] is done because of that which the LORD did unto me when I came forth out of Egypt."[4] Jewish tradition has identified two commandments from this verse in Exodus. First is the commandment to teach children about the Exodus from Egypt. This exhortation is repeated four times, thus establishing the teaching of new generations as the primary task of every Seder. The second commandment comes from the phrase, "I came forth out of Egypt." Because the first-person voice is used, rabbis have noted that every participant at the Seder should feel that they were personally redeemed from Egypt. Every time God's people are liberated,

---

4. Exodus 13:8.

it becomes part of the Passover story; therefore, the Seder is a time to recount other instances where the Lord has delivered his people. For instance, the Jews would remember the end of the Holocaust, Mormons would remember the miracle of the sea gulls, and Nephites would remember the leading of Lehi through the wilderness. When miracles of deliverance are recited during the Passover ceremony, generations are bound together as they praise the mercy of God.

There are several parts of the Book of Mormon that may be linked with this tradition. For examples, see Mosiah 27:16, Alma 29:11-12 and Alma 5:4-7. But the example most directly tied to Passover is in Alma 36:28-29. Speaking to his son, Alma says, "I will praise him [God] forever, for he has brought our fathers out of Egypt, and he has swallowed up the Egyptians in the Red Sea; and he led them by his power into the promised land; yea, and he has delivered them out of bondage and captivity from time to time. Yea, and he has also brought our fathers out of the land of Jerusalem; and he has also, by his everlasting power, delivered them out of bondage and captivity, from time to time even down to the present day; and I have always retained in remembrance their captivity; yea and ye also ought to retain in remembrance as I have done, their captivity."[5] This passage would fit easily into any Passover Haggadah. Alma, speaking to his son, recounts the deliverance in Egypt, then relates it to other miracles his son is familiar with, ending with an exhortation to remember the mercy of the Lord. Of course, Passover is never specifically identified, but the similarities are striking, nonetheless. In this gentle admonition, Alma is keeping the ancient commandment to teach his son about the deliverance of God.

---

5. Alma 36:28-29.

Elijah's Return
and the Kirtland Temple

One Latter-day Passover is vitally important to Latter-day Saints. The Old Testament prophet Malachi recorded the prophetic promise that, "I will send you Elijah the prophet, before the coming of the great and dreadful day of the Lord."[6] This verse of scripture is the origin of Jewish tradition designating Elijah as the forerunner of the Messiah. Elijah's return is considered by Jews to be the first sign of the long-awaited Messianic era—a time when light and truth will be showered upon the earth preceding the Messiah's arrival. As the Haggadah explains, "This man of mystery became associated with the End of Days, with the Messianic hopes of our people. The prophet Malachi promised that Elijah would come to turn the hearts of parents to children, and the hearts of children to parents, and to announce the coming of the Messiah when all mankind would celebrate freedom."[7]

Joseph Smith also taught of the relationship between the return of Elijah and the coming of the Messiah. He explained, "The spirit of Elias is first, Elijah second, and Messiah last. Elias is a forerunner to prepare the way, and the spirit and power of Elijah is to come after, holding the keys of power, building the Temple to the capstone, placing the seals of the Melchizedek Priesthood upon the house of Israel, and making all things ready; then Messiah comes to His Temple, which is last of all."[8]

On Easter Sunday in 1836, during the Passover festival when Jewish families around the world opened doors and

---

6. Malachi 4:5.
7. Bronstein and Baskin, *op. cit.,* 68.
8. Smith, *Teachings of the Prophet Joseph Smith,* 340.

invited him to enter, Elijah appeared to the Prophet Joseph Smith and Oliver Cowdery in the newly dedicated Kirtland Temple. There he restored sealing keys that permit families to be bound together eternally.

The importance of this date is underscored by an amazing astronomical coincidence that links the date of the Savior's resurrection with Elijah's return in this last dispensation. The Jewish lunar calendar and our modern solar calendar do not often align, but Elijah's return in 1836 occurred not only during Passover week, as anticipated by the Jews, but also on an Easter Sunday calendrically similar to the proposed date of the Savior's resurrection, being both April 3 on the Gregorian calendar and 16 Nisan on the Hebrew calendar. Mormon scholar John P. Pratt said, "The Easter of 1836 was calendrically the most similar in history to the Easter of A.D. 33. And if the earth's orbit continues unchanged, that Easter should retain this distinction for another three thousand years. The year 1836 was the only such occurrence in the nineteenth century!"[9]

This is obviously much more than a remarkable coincidence. Elijah's return occurred on the exact anniversary of the resurrection, which emphasizes the essential and holy nature of the priesthood restoration. Modern-day scripture teaches us just how important Elijah's return was. The Doctrine and Covenants says, "The Prophet Elijah was to plant in the hearts of the children the promises made to their fathers, foreshadowing the great work to be done in the temples of the Lord in the dispensation of the fullness of times, for the redemption of the dead . . . lest the whole earth be utterly wasted at his com-

9. John P. Pratt, "The Restoration of Priesthood Keys on Easter 1836, Part 2," *Ensign,* July 1985, 55.

ing."[10] The whole purpose of this earth experience for mankind is to exalt families, an impossible goal without the priesthood keys restored by Elijah. Because of the sealing power, families can exist eternally, and priesthood power can bless all generations of humanity.

At his return, Elijah declared, "Therefore, the keys of this dispensation are committed into your hands; and by this ye may know that the great and dreadful day of the Lord is near, even at the doors."[11] The coming of Elijah truly marked a time when light and truth were showered upon the earth as never before. The return of Elijah on the Jewish Passover bears eloquent testimony that the Law of Moses foreshadowed the Lord's death and resurrection in the meridian of time, as well as his miracles in latter days. How marvelous it is to stand at this pinnacle of history, a time ancient seers foretold, and watch prophesies from ages past fulfilled before our very eyes!

Herald of the Second Coming

Not only does Passover symbolize events of the past, but it is also a precursor to Christ's Second Coming. To understand this, we must review the Jewish prophecies of the Messiah. In many ways, the time of King David represents the pinnacle of Jewish history. During his reign, Israel was united under a righteous monarch, and the nation enjoyed freedom. However, shortly after Solomon's death, the nation was split into the Northern Kingdom and the Southern Kingdom. Then, beginning in 722 B.C., Israel was gradually conquered by its enemies and was never unified and controlled by the

---

10. D&C 138:47-49.
11. D&C 110:16.

Jewish people from then until the state of Israel was created in 1948![12]

The Lord promised King David that someday his heir would rule over united Israel once again. "Thine house and thy kingdom shall be established for ever before thee: thy throne shall be established for ever."[13] In ancient Israel, prophets, high priests, and kings were anointed and often called "messiah." But "The Messiah" refers to the rightful ruler and promised king who would throw off Israel's oppressors and reclaim the throne of his father, King David. For instance, one Messianic prophesy states, "I will commit thy government into his hand: and the key of the house of David will I lay upon his shoulder and they shall hang upon him all the glory of his father's house."[14] Thus, when a blind man called Jesus "Son of David," he was in fact affirming that Jesus was the Messiah and promised ruler.[15]

As centuries passed and the Jews were scattered by nation after nation, their hope for the Messiah to deliver them from their enemies and restore their homeland intensified. Throughout scripture, prophets encouraged the people to trust that eventually the conquering Messiah would save them. For example, Isaiah wrote of the Messiah's coming, "For unto us a child is born, unto us a son is given and the government shall be upon his shoulder . . . of the increase of his government and peace there shall be no end, upon the throne of David, and

---

12. Although the Maccabees succeeded in reestablishing Jewish rule after the revolt of 168-165 B.C., they ruled under the control of the Greeks and then the Romans. The State of Israel was established in 1948, but the country was not completely controlled by the Israelis until after the war of 1967. For more information, see Wylen.

13. 2 Samuel 7:16.

14. Isaiah 22:21-24.

15. Matthew 20:30.

upon his kingdom, to order it and to establish it with judgment and with justice from henceforth even forever."[16]

Juxtaposed with those scriptures speaking of the Messiah as a political savior are other scriptures that describe the Messiah as a humble servant who will bring spiritual redemption to the world. Isaiah described the Messiah in the following terms: "He is despised and rejected of men, a man of sorrows, and acquainted with grief . . . But he was wounded for our transgressions, he was bruised for our iniquities: the chastisement of our peace was upon him; and with his stripes we are healed. He was oppressed, and he was afflicted, yet he opened not his mouth: he is brought as a lamb to the slaughter, and as a sheep before her shearers is dumb, so he openeth not his mouth."[17] These two views of the Messiah—political sovereign and suffering redeemer—seem irreconcilable.

This paradox gives us greater compassion and insight into why some Jews rejected Jesus and why even the disciples despaired at his death. If Jesus of Nazareth was really the Messiah, they expected him to reclaim David's throne, unify the country, and reestablish political freedom. Zachariah, the father of John the Baptist, had taught, while speaking with inspiration: "He spake by the mouth of his holy prophets, which have been since the world began, that we should be saved from our enemies, and from the hand of all that hate us."[18] Yet when Jesus was crucified, the Jews were still under Roman rule, their political situation as grim as ever. It is easy to see why many felt Jesus could not have been the Messiah they awaited.

In our day, it is apparent that Isaiah's dualistic prophecies were accurate and inspired, for he wrote of a Messiah who would come more than once. The two arrivals would be as

---

16. Isaiah 9:6-7.
17. Isaiah 53:3-6.
18. Luke 1:70-71.

different as night from day. When the Messiah first came to earth, he was humble, meek, and submissive; but at his Second Coming, he will be heralded Sovereign Ruler and glorious God. The first advent was ignominiously begun in a lowly stable; but all flesh will witness his Second Coming, as every knee bows and every tongue confesses his glory.

Passover anticipates the ultimate freedom enjoyed by the righteous during the millennium. Isaiah foresaw this time and described, "[The Messiah has] broken the staff of the wicked and the scepter of the rulers. The whole earth is at rest and is quiet: they break forth into singing. Then shall his yoke depart from off them, and his burden depart from off their shoulders . . . I will gather all nations and tongues and they shall come, and see my glory."[19] At this time, Zion will rejoice because "the Holy One of Israel [will be] in the midst of thee."[20] The time spoken of is, of course, when the Savior reigns upon the earth. On that day, the earth will be freed from death, sorrow, sin, and hatred. The earth shall appear as the garden of the Eden, and "they shall not hurt nor destroy in all my holy mountain: for the earth shall be full of the knowledge of the LORD, as the waters cover the sea."[21]

The act of pouring a fifth cup in the Seder symbolizes this promise of the Lord, yet to be fulfilled. It is an affirmation of faith that the Lord will keep his promise and return with freedom one last time. The cup of Elijah reflects the ancient tradition that Elijah would return at Passover time. The promise of the fifth cup is "I will bring you into the land." The land spoken of in this scripture refers first to the land of Israel, and metaphorically to Zion, the kingdom of God established on

19. Isaiah 14:7, 25; 66:18.
20. Isaiah 12:6.
21. Isaiah 11:9.

the millennial earth. As one Jewish scholar noted, "[Elijah's cup] reaches out in spirit for that ultimate glory, promised through the prophets and described by the rabbis: the Messianic age, the end of subjugation for all, encapsulated in the words 'Next year in Jerusalem!'"[22]

Judah and Joseph Reunited

Through the restoration of the gospel, we are blessed to know that Elijah returned, as prophesied. Consistent with ancient and modern scripture, signs preceding the Second Coming of the Messiah appear all around us. As events unfold, armies will amass around the Jews. Once again the Jews will be fighting their oppressors, and they will be losing. At that moment, faced with certain captivity, the long-awaited political Messiah will at last appear. He will set foot upon the Mount of Olives and it will wrench apart. The enemies will be destroyed, and in wonder the Jewish survivors will look upon their deliverer, this glorious being foretold for centuries of time. LDS authors Ann and Bernard Madsen described, "Then the Jews will gather around their Messiah in the deepest adoration, but they will be puzzled by the wounds in his hands. Gradually it will dawn on them that this is none other than Jesus of Nazareth. From that moment on, both Jews and Christians will worship the same Messiah."[23]

Heathen nations will say to the Jews, "We will go with you: for we have heard that God is with you."[24] At that day, Passover prophecies will be complete and the house of Israel will be reunited. Once again, we will walk hand in hand with

---

22. Bronstein and Baskin, *op. cit.,* 11.

23. Ann N. Madsen and Barnard M. Madsen, "Judah through the Centuries," *Ensign,* January 1982, 20.

24. Zechariah 8:22-23.

our brothers and sisters of the house of Judah. "And the time cometh that he shall manifest himself unto all nations, both unto the Jews and also unto the Gentiles; and after he has manifested himself unto the Jews and also unto the Gentiles, then he shall manifest himself unto the Gentiles and also unto the Jews, and the last shall be first, and the first shall be last."[25]

Latter-day Saints have been called to play a role in preparing the earth for this long-awaited time. Ann and Bernard Madsen wrote, "It is clear that we of Joseph need to understand more about our brothers and sisters of Judah: to understand that we have a common father, a common heritage, and a common destiny."[26] That common destiny is tied to the Passover symbol of the Zeroah, or shankbone. Its presence on the Passover plate is a reminder that the Lord's arm of mercy is still stretched out, and He will come to usher in the era of millennial peace. This destiny is also anticipated by the Haggadah's concluding line, "Next year in Jerusalem! Next year may all be free!" This does not mean Jerusalem as we know it, but the rebuilt Jerusalem of the Second Coming, where a millennial Temple will stand. When we repeat this phrase, we affirm our longing for that day. We live for it, hope for it, and strive to be worthy to stand on that day when the Messiah descends. As Ezra Taft Benson taught, "We look forward to the day of fulfillment of God's promise when 'the house of Judah shall walk with the house of Israel.'"[27] Perhaps my beloved teacher, Rabbi David Rosen, said it best. Teaching students in Israel about this principle, he said,

---

25. (1 Nephi 13:41-42).

26. Madsen, *Op. cit.* See also 2 Nephi 29:5.

27. Ezra Taft Benson, "A Message to Judah from Joseph," *Ensign,* December 1976, 67. Scripture in quote is Jeremiah 3:18.

"When Messiah comes, you and I will go hand in hand to meet him. And then we will ask him if he has been here before. Regardless of his answer, I believe he will welcome us both if we strive diligently to serve God today."[28]

Perhaps at that day, the world will celebrate one beautiful Passover/Sacrament service in unity, with the Savior at the head.

28. Rabbi David Rosen, lecture given at Brigham Young University's Jerusalem Center for Near Eastern Studies, May 1994.

Part Two

Celebrating a Latter-day Saint Passover

7
Organizing Your Seder

In Part One, we examined the history and symbolism of the Passover festival. Part Two provides the necessary information to help you and your family create a Latter-day Saint version of the Seder. The Passover Seder can be thought of as a religious pageant, directed by a leader following the Haggadah as the script for the evening. The service changes slightly each year, according to the interest and ages of the participants.

Follow the Leader

The first step in organizing your Passover evening is selecting one adult to be the Seder leader. Traditionally the Seder is led by the father of the family, but anyone can fulfill this responsibility. The Passover Plate with the symbolic foods is placed at the head of the table, directly in front of the leader, so he or she can hold up each of the items as they are discussed.

Tailor the Script

The leader should read through the Haggadah script well ahead of time. During the Seder, certain sections of the text are be read aloud by the leader, but the remaining stories, quotes, and scriptures are divided among other participants to read. The leader decides who reads each part. Interest is piqued when everyone has a part to play, so carefully consider how each guest can be involved. As the leader, you may choose to tailor the Haggadah for your family's particular needs. Feel free to adjust the text to the interest level of your audience. The tailoring of the text is firmly rooted in the Jewish tradition—it is said that no two Seders should ever be the same. The Passover dinner should be a time when children and adults alike are comfortable asking questions. As one Haggadah taught, "Encourage informal participation, questioning, and spirited discussion. Each family is different . . . the aim is a celebration, serious yet relaxed, and filled with gaiety and drama." [1]

Above all, the Seder is a time for families and friends to discuss the gospel together. If your group will consist mainly of older children and adults, you may want to photocopy the Haggadah so all in attendance can follow along. When I lead a Seder, I use highlighters to make a personalized copy for each participant, clearly marking the sections he or she will read. I then note who will read each part on my own script, turning mine into a master copy so I can call on each participant in turn.

An alternative idea is to make one photocopy of the Haggadah, number the quotes you would like read, and then cut those sections into strips. Simply pass out the strips to your guests and call for each number in turn.

Plan the Service

A few sections of the text call for preparation. For instance, at one point, a child asks four questions. This offers an opportunity to help small children feel involved. Assist the child or children as they prepare to ask the questions, so they won't be nervous when their time comes. If you don't have any children participating, an adult may read the questions.

The service concludes with a hymn. If you have any musically talented family members, request their assistance with

_____

1. Bronstein and Baskin, *op, cit.,* 14.

singing or playing a musical instrument. If your group is not musically inspired, CDs were invented just for you. A list of recommended songs, including fun Passover songs for young children, is provided in Chapter 11.

Prepare the Home

One commandment associated with this holiday is found in Exodus. "Unleavened bread shall be eaten seven days; and there shall no leavened bread be seen with thee, neither shall there be leaven seen with thee in all thy quarters."[2] For seven days after Passover, no yeast is eaten in the Jewish home. On the most basic level, the unleavened bread represents the hasty departure of the Israelites from Egypt. Legend says that they fled so quickly there was no time for their bread to rise, so they carried the dough on baking trays upon their backs. As they fled, the rising sun cooked the dough into flat, hard cakes—the first matzah. But on a more symbolic level, yeast causes bread to raise through a process of decomposition and fermentation; therefore, leaven represents decay or sin.

The scriptural command that no leaven be found in the home is taken very literally, so the house is scoured from top to bottom. As one Jewish author, Herman Wouk, recounted, "The rabbinic regulations for carrying out this law recall the stringency of hospital antisepsis. Jewish housewives, following the rules in all generations with great strictness, have evolved a sort of sacred spring-cleaning in the week before the holiday, meticulous to the last cranny, to the pockets of clothes, to the dark corners of cellars and closets."[3] Today rabbis have determined that in addition to yeast, any foods

---

2. Exodus 13:7.
3. Wouk, *op. cit.,* 57.

that can become subject to leavening are not kosher[4] for Passover (this includes flour, cereal, bread, and crackers). All leavened products are given to neighbors, put into storage, or thrown out. Many homes have special dishes, utensils, cookware, and even ovens that are free from leaven and used only during the holiday.

On the evening before the first day of Passover, all leaven must be gone from the home. This fulfills the commandment, "The first day ye shall put away leaven out of your houses."[5] As darkness falls, a dramatic search for leaven takes place. At various spots throughout the home, parents hide pieces of bread. In the dark, the children search for them by the light of a candle (or flashlight). The forbidden bread is gathered in a bag and burned. The home is then pronounced sanctified and ready for Passover.

In the LDS home, where we are not attempting to abide by the Law of Moses, most of these preparations may be considered unnecessary (although they might provide a good excuse to clean house). Whether we participate or not, we can learn much from the spiritual application of these traditions, for they are rich indeed. As we think of the Israelites fleeing Egypt, we learn that we must flee from our sins and hasten to Christ. As we prepare for this holiday, we can remember that our homes must be free from destructive influences. We cleanse them and keep them pure and holy, dedicated to the Lord. And when we eat the unleavened bread, we recall that our Savior is the pure bread of life, free from all sin. You may want to discuss the Jewish practice of scouring the home with

---

4. The term "kosher" means that a food item has been prepared according to Old Testament dietary laws.
5. Exodus 12:15.

your family before this special day and ask family members to help keep their relations pure and sweet in anticipation.

Although the preparations required of Jewish households may seem extensive, they serve an important function of helping the family members prepare spiritually for the occasion. How can children help but notice the home scoured, the hard matzah eaten in place of bread, and the dramatic search for leaven by candlelight?

Herman Wouk wrote, "The children who go around with their father the evening before Passover by candlelight, searching out the last scraps of leaven for burning, never forget the experience."[6] Although the LDS home's preparation may vary significantly, we can also help our families gain the most from a sacred Easter day.

Family Home Evening Ideas

Consider holding a special family home evening the week before Easter. You may want to read the scriptural account of Jesus' last supper, death, and resurrection throughout the week. Discuss the principles of the Atonement with your family and help them to understand that Easter is a day to remember the death and resurrection of the Savior. Emphasize that the Atonement makes it possible for us to repent from our sins, overcome death, and live with our families forever.

Well before Easter, discuss your plan to hold a Passover Seder with your family. It may be appropriate to read the story of Passover together in Exodus 12. Explain that years before Christ came to the earth, God gave His people commandments and festivals to help prepare them for the Savior's coming and that the Law of Moses was given to the ancient

---

6. Wouk, *op. cit.,* 57.

prophets to teach them of Christ. Tell your family that on Easter you would like to celebrate one of these ancient festivals that prophesied of Christ. Although observing Passover is no longer required, the tradition still has much to teach us about our Savior.

Because the Passover Seder deals with so many symbols of slavery and freedom, it is essential that participants understand that without the Atonement of Christ, we are in bondage to sin and death. Because of his sacrifice, we are free to live both spiritually and physically. Even young children can understand this idea through the use of object lessons. For instance, you can use string to represent sin. Show your children that when sin is wound around our wrists, it takes away our freedom to move. Jesus suffered and died for our sins, which gave him the power to cut through this sin and set us free.

Enlist your family's help in the Seder preparations. Let them know that everyone will be involved. In one section of the service, children are sent to search out bread that has been hidden. When they find this afikoman, they are given a prize. Presented in an enthusiastic way, this treasure hunt will interest children of all ages. Children can also help prepare the meal. Recipes for the symbolic foods are simple enough for children to follow with minimal adult supervision.

Whether your preparations are extensive or minimal, prayerfully consider ways you can help your family to gain as much as possible from the Easter/Passover celebration. Your preparation will be greatly rewarded. One rabbi recommended, "The Seder . . . is a religious drama of the highest significance. Preparation is needed not only by those who prepare the dinner and conduct the Seder service but also by others who attend."[7]

---

7. Bronstein and Baskin, *op. cit.,* 14.

Passover Preparation Checklist

- Choose a leader.
- Photocopy the script and divide the reading parts.
- Ask children to read the four questions.
- Arrange for music.
- Do some spiritual or physical spring-cleaning.
- Explain the Seder to your family members and enlist their help with preparation.
- Carefully consider ways to help your family best prepare for Easter, such as having a special Family Home Evening or object lessons.
- Read scriptures illustrating these principles. Possibilities include:

  Exodus 12:5-14 (Passover is instituted)
  Jacob 4:4-5 (Law of Moses symbolizes Christ)
  2 Nephi 11:4 (Law of Moses symbolizes Christ)
  Alma 25:15-16 (Law of Moses symbolizes Christ)
  3 Nephi 15:3-10 (Christ explains that Law is fulfilled)
  Alma 34:13-14 (Law of Moses symbolizes Christ)
  1 Corinthians 5:7 (Christ is our Passover)
  John 20:1-17 (Christ appears to Mary at the tomb)
  Mosiah 15:8-9, 23 (Christ breaks the bands of death)
  Mosiah 16:7-9 (Christ has conquered death)
  D&C 138:12-17, 50 (Rejoicing at resurrection)
  Romans 8:21 (Christ offers "glorious liberty")

8
Planning the Meal

The Passover Seder consists of three parts: the portion before the meal, the meal itself, and the readings after dinner. The Seder is basically a service wrapped around a festive supper. Like many things connected with Passover, the dinner is as individual as the family who celebrates it. The meal may be a simple affair or a lavish banquet. You can decide what fits your family's needs best. If you wish to continue with Easter traditions, feel free to wrap your Seder service around your customary Easter meal. The only necessities are the symbolic foods discussed in Chapter Nine. However, if you wish to celebrate an authentic Passover, make use of the following traditional Jewish recipes.

Because these recipes are made with unleavened products, they are kosher. The matzah flour used in these recipes can be purchased from any grocery store around Passover time. Regular flour or breadcrumbs may be substituted, but the dish will not be kosher, since regular flour contains leavening agents. Regardless of what you serve, have it ready ahead of time to save tension on a day that is supposed to be peaceful.

Matzah (Unleavened Bread)

3 cups matzah meal (or flour)
pinch of salt   water

Preheat oven to 400 degrees. Mix all ingredients and knead until dough is soft and fine. Divide dough into 3 parts. Roll out thin like piecrust. Set on lightly oiled [vegetable oil only, to be kosher] cookie sheet, and use a fork to lightly puncture the dough. Bake until lightly browned. Turn matzah over and bake until brown. Cover and place at Seder table.

Charoset (the Mortar)

Charoset can be made in many different ways. It often includes diced apples, walnuts, almonds, dates, figs, raisins, dried apricots, grape juice, cinnamon, and honey. One recipe follows, but feel free to adapt it to your family's taste.

2 green apples, peeled and chopped

1/2 cup nuts, chopped   1/2 tsp. cinnamon

1/2 cup chopped fruit

(bananas, raisins, figs, and/or dried apricots)

1/4 cup orange juice   1/4 cup honey

Mix all ingredients together. Chill.

Herb-Rubbed Leg of Lamb

A note about serving lamb: Because the destruction of the Temple made it impossible for a sacrificial Passover lamb to be served at the meal, most Jews do not to serve lamb at the Seder. But for LDS families, serving lamb helps recreate a Seder meal similar to the one that Jesus ate. This recipe will make the best lamb you have ever had!

one 7-lb. leg of lamb

the juice of one fresh lemon

4 tbsp. fresh parsley, snipped

2 tsp. dried basil

1/2 tsp. onion salt

1 tsp. crushed rosemary

1/2 tsp. pepper

1/2 tsp. garlic salt

5 cloves of garlic, slivered

Preheat the oven to 325 degrees. Trim the fat from the meat and cut 1/2-inch-wide slits into the roast at 1-inch intervals. Brush fresh lemon juice over the meat surface and into the pockets. Mix together all spices in a bowl, and rub the spices all over meat and into pockets. Stuff pockets with garlic slivers. Place meat (fat side up) in a shallow roasting pan. Roast for 3 hours. Remove from oven, cover with foil, and let stand for 15 minutes before carving.

Cucumber and Tomato Salad

Variations of this light, refreshing salad are served throughout Israel.

3 English-style cucumbers

7 large tomatoes

3/4 cup fresh basil, chopped

1/3 cup green onions, chopped

1 cup plain yogurt

1 cup balsamic vinaigrette salad dressing

salt and pepper to taste

Slice cucumbers and tomatoes into a large bowl. Add basil and green onions. In a separate smaller bowl, mix yogurt and salad dressing and beat until smooth. Pour dressing mixture on top of cucumbers and tomatoes. Add salt and pepper to taste. The salad should be prepared at least one hour before serving, to allow flavors to marinate.

Vegetable Kugel

Kugel is a tasty casserole made from potatoes or noodles.

1 (12 oz.) package thin egg noodles (use Passover noodles for a kosher dish)

1 onion, diced

1 package sliced mushrooms

1 zucchini, sliced

4 carrots, sliced

2 cans cream of chicken soup

1/2 cup sour cream

5 eggs

1 cup matzo meal (or bread crumbs)

1/2 cup mozzarella cheese

salt and pepper to taste

paprika to taste

Preheat oven to 350 degrees. Grease a 9" x 13" baking dish. Cook egg noodles in boiling water according to directions on package. While pasta is cooking, heat oil in a skillet over medium heat. Add all vegetables and sauté until barely tender. In large mixing bowl combine cooked pasta, sautéed vegetables, matzah meal, soup, sour cream, cheese, and eggs. Mix thoroughly and season with salt and pepper to taste. Pour into baking dish and sprinkle with paprika. Bake 40 minutes, until top is crisp and golden.

Matzah Ball Soup

This soup is a Passover standard.

1 large carrot, cut into 1-inch pieces	1 tbsp. salt
1 large onion, quartered	1/4 tsp. white pepper
1 tbsp. parsley flakes	2 chicken bouillon cubes
2 stalks celery, chopped	2 quarts cold water

In large soup pot combine all ingredients. Bring to a boil. Reduce heat and simmer while preparing matzah balls.

Matzah Balls

2 tbsp. oil	2 eggs, beaten
2 tbsp. melted butter	4 tbsp. soup broth
1 tsp. parsley flakes	1 tsp. salt
1/4 cup minced onion	1/2 tsp. pepper
3/4 cup matzah meal	

Mix together matzah meal, parsley flakes, salt, and pepper. In a separate bowl, combine eggs, oil, butter, onion, and soup broth. Mix just enough of the matzah mixture into the egg mixture to make it hold together. Chill in refrigerator for 20 minutes. Using your hands, form the mixture into golf-ball sized matzah balls. Place matzah balls into the boiling soup. Cover the pot and cook 30 to 40 minutes. DO NOT remove the cover from the pot while it is cooking!

Gefilte¹ Fish

These fish patties are usually served at room temperature, but they may be served hot as well.

1 1/2 lbs. pike, carp, or other
    white fish fillets, cut into
    2-inch pieces
1/4 cup matzah meal
2 large eggs, separated

1 medium onion,
    finely chopped
1 tsp. salt
1/4 tsp. pepper
2 quarts boiling water
    or stock

In a food processor, chop fish a few pieces at a time until fine and smooth. Add matzo meal, egg yolks, onion, salt, and pepper, mixing briefly after each addition. In a separate bowl, whip egg whites until stiff peaks form. Gently fold into fish mixture. Form the mixture into oval patties (put a little oil on hands to keep mixture from sticking). Gently place the patties into boiling stock or water. Cover. Return to boil. Remove cover, reduce heat, and simmer for 1 hour.

Potato Latkes²

These delicious potato pancakes are always popular.

6 medium grated potatoes
1 cup onion
1/2 cup grated carrots
1/4 cup matzah meal

1/2 tsp. salt
1/4 tsp. pepper
4 egg whites
pan spray

---

1. Pronounced gu-FIL-tu.
2. Pronounced LAHT-kuz.

Preheat oven to 375 degrees. Peel and grate the potatoes and vegetables. Put them in a large bowl and add the remaining ingredients. Mix well. Spray muffin tins with pan spray and put 1/4 cup of the potato mixture in each muffin cup. Bake for 45 minutes and remove. Flip latkes onto a cookie sheet. Cook for 10 more minutes on the reverse side until crisp. Serve with applesauce.

Stuffed Zucchinis

This delicious vegetable dish makes a nice accompaniment for any Passover meal.

4 zucchinis, cut in half lengthwise

1 large onion, finely chopped

1/4 cup vegetable juice

1 tsp. parsley

2 cloves chopped garlic

4 tbsp. matzah meal

1/2 cup grated mozzarella cheese

Preheat oven to 375 degrees. Scoop out pulp from zucchini halves. Heat zucchini pulp, onion, vegetable juice, and spices in a pan for 5 minutes or until vegetables are tender. Add matzah meal and mix well. Restuff zucchini with mixture. Place in a baking dish with a little vegetable juice on bottom. Top with grated mozzarella cheese and bake for 45 minutes or until zucchini shells are soft.

Acorn Squash with Apple Stuffing

This delicious vegetable makes a nice accompaniment for any Passover meal.

3 acorn squashes   cinnamon to taste
3 tbsp. melted butter   1/2 cup water
salt to taste

Stuffing:

1/3 cup raisins   5 tbsp. butter
1/3 cup grape juice   1/3 cup brown sugar
4 medium apples   1 1/2 tbsp. lemon juice

Preheat oven to 350 degrees. Halve the squashes and scoop out seeds. Trim undersides so halves will sit flat. Brush cut surfaces with melted margarine and sprinkle with salt and cinnamon. Place face down in baking pan. Pour 1/2 cup water or enough to just cover the bottom of pan. Bake 30 minutes.

While squash is baking, soak raisins in grape juice to plump. Chop apples into 1/2-inch cubes, peeled or unpeeled. In a small pan, melt the butter and add the apples. Cook 3 to 5 minutes, or until slightly tender. Stir in sugar and lemon juice.

When squash has cooked 30 minutes, turn them face up. Drain the raisins and add to the apple mixture. Fill squash cavities with the raisins and apple mixture. Cover and bake 20 to 30 minutes more, or until tender.

Passover Chocolate Nut Torte

This recipe proves that Passover dishes can be decadent.

6 eggs, separated	1 cup chopped walnuts
1 1/2 cups sugar	1/2 cup matzah meal
4 oz. semi-sweet chocolate, grated	
1 yellow delicious apple, peeled and grated	

Preheat oven to 350 degrees. Beat egg yolks with sugar until lemon-colored and thick. Gently stir in nuts, chocolate, apples, and matzah meal. In a separate bowl, beat the egg whites until they form stiff peaks. Fold egg whites into egg yolk mixture gently but thoroughly. Turn mixture into a greased 9-inch cake pan. Bake 55 minutes or until cake springs back when pressed lightly with your fingers. Cool in pan.

Apple Cake

This is similar to coffee cake.

Cake:

3 eggs	1/3 cup vegetable oil
3/4 cup sugar	3/4 cup matzah meal
5 Granny Smith apples, peeled and sliced	

Topping:

1/2 cup sugar	1/3 cup chopped walnuts
2 tsp. cinnamon	

Preheat oven to 350°. In a medium-sized mixing bowl, beat the eggs with the sugar and vegetable oil until the mixture is light. Add the matzah meal and mix well. Pour half of the mixture into a lightly greased 8- or 9-inch square baking pan. Distribute half the apples over the batter. Pour the remaining batter over the apples and cover with rest of the apples. Combine the topping ingredients in a small bowl and sprinkle over the top of the mixtures. Bake for approximately 1 1/2 hours.

9
Preparing the Table and Passover Plate

Set the table in the most festive manner—after all, this is a joyous feast! The following items are necessary:

Two white candles are placed in front of the matriarch of the house. She lights them at the beginning of the ceremony. (Don't forget the matches.)

Three pieces of matzah are placed at the center of the table, with napkins between each piece. Additional matzah should be available to eat with the meal. Matzah is sold in boxes in nearly every grocery store at Passover time. Make sure you get it before Passover, however, because it is difficult to find afterwards. Luckily, matzah stays fresh for a very long time, so may be purchased well ahead of time. Or you can make your own (see Chapter 8 for recipe).

Grape Juice. The traditional Jewish Seder is celebrated with wine, but even health-conscious Jews have started using grape juice (especially since four cups are consumed during the evening!). Feel free to use any red juice you like, but bottles of sparkling grape juice add a special ambiance. The cups do not need to be filled all the way—just a few swallows in each glass will do.

A few bowls of salt water should be on the table within reach of all guests.

A place for Elijah should be set. An extra cup will be filled with grape juice at a certain point in the Seder. Elijah's cup should be the finest one on the table.

Passover Plate set with the symbolic foods.

In front of each guest should be a *dinner plate* and *a glass for grape juice.*

Preparing the Passover Plate

The special Passover plate displays all of the symbolic foods. The Seder plate is a very special part of the service. Most Jewish homes have china platters that were specifically made for this purpose. If you want one of these beautiful plates for your Seder table, it can be purchased at Jewish stores or online at www.judaism.com and www.mazeltov-pages.com. Otherwise, feel free to use a plain white plate, or use the following instructions to make your own Seder plate. Involve your kids and create a true heirloom.

Making a Seder Plate: To make a Seder plate, you need a white plate and supplies for writing. If you choose a plate made of china or glass, special permanent paints for glassware are available at craft stores. With a plastic plate you can use fabric paint pens, permanent markers, or acrylics sealed with glaze. Simply paint or write the names of each symbolic food around the edge of your plate in Hebrew or English (see diagram). The five words written on the plate are: maror/bitter herbs, karpas/parsley, beytzah/egg, zeroah/bone, and charoset/mortar. In the center of the plate, write *Pesach* or *Passover.*

The Five Food Symbols on the Passover Plate

(For more information on the food symbols and how they relate to Christ, see Chapter 4.)

Maror/Bitter herbs: Any bitter herb may be used, including bite-sized pieces of radish, hearts of romaine, or

Arranging the Passover Plate

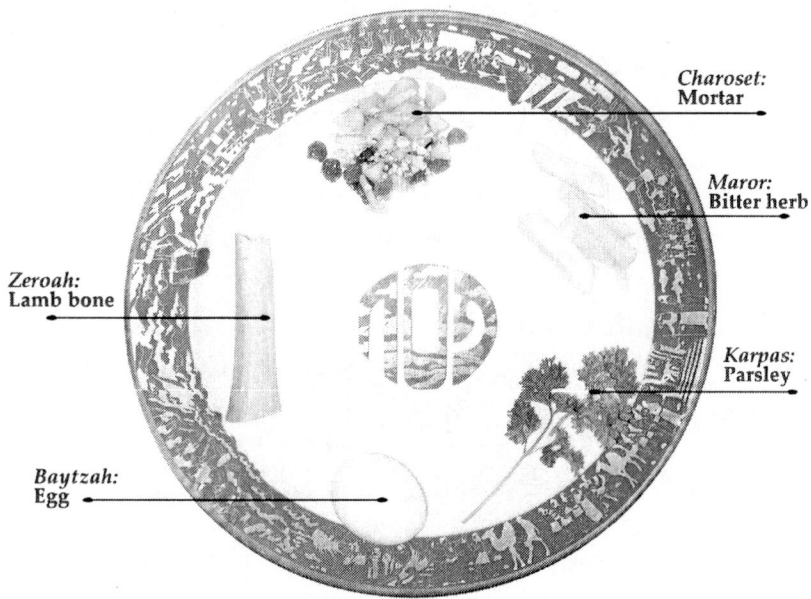

Charoset: Mortar

Maror: Bitter herb

Zeroah: Lamb bone

Karpas: Parsley

Baytzah: Egg

pieces of horseradish root (my personal favorite—the symbol of slavery should sting!). To use horseradish, purchase a whole root from the grocery store. Peel it and chop into small pieces. Careful—it is potent! The bitter herbs represent the harsh and grinding bitterness that fills a life of bondage. Spiritually, it reminds us of the pain we feel when we are in the bondage of sin.

Karpas/Parsley: Parsley is the green herb most commonly used, but other leafy green herbs may be used as well. The parsley reminds us that new, green life comes out of the blackness of winter—foreshadowing the promise of the resurrection after the darkness of death. The karpas is dipped in salt water to remind us of the tears of bondage.

Beytzah/Roasted Egg: The egg on the Seder plate is supposed to be roasted. Simply hard-boil it first (so it doesn't
explode!), then broil it in the oven until it turns brown. When
the Jewish Temple was destroyed, a few decades after the
death of Jesus, it became impossible to fulfill the required
Passover sacrifices, so the egg is placed on the plate to remind
us of ancient sacrifices no longer performed. The egg is yet
another symbol of life renewing itself and of triumph over
death. The egg is dipped in salt water to remind us that life
was bought with tears.

Zeroah/Shank bone: Traditionally, the Passover lamb had
to be slaughtered at the Temple in Jerusalem. After the
destruction of the Temple, it became impossible to observe
this festival commandment so it is now customary not to eat
lamb at Passover, because it cannot be prepared at the Temple. Instead, a shank bone is placed on the Passover plate to
remember the lamb that was sacrificed. Any bone can be used
on the plate; even a small stick can play the part. The bone is
the greatest symbol to Latter-day Saints, because it points to
the sacrifice of the holy Lamb of God, "the Lamb slain from
the foundation of the world." [1]

Charoset/Mortar: Charoset is a sweet mixture of honey,
nuts, and fruit. It recalls the mortar that our ancestors were
forced to make for Pharaoh. Although it represents slave
labor, its sweetness reminds us of the hope for release. The
charoset is eaten after the bitter herbs, reminding us that only
after we know the bitterness of bondage can we truly appreciate the sweetness of freedom. Charoset can be made in
many different ways. One recipe is found in Chapter 8.

---

1. Revelation 13:8.

Table Checklist

- Two white candles and matches
- Matzah (unleavened bread)
- Grape juice
- Bowls of salt water
- A cup for Elijah
- A Passover plate with the following symbolic foods:

    Bitter herbs
    Parsley
    Roasted Egg
    Bone
    Charoset (fruit/nut mixture)

10

A Latter-day Saint's Haggadah[1]

The Seder consists of three parts: the service before dinner, the dinner, and readings afterwards. The following is an overview of the whole ceremony:

Opening: Welcome guests and sanctify the day. Light candles, offer a prayer, and pour the first cup of grape juice.

Wash hands: Pass a bowl of water to wash hands.

Karpas: Bless and eat the parsley.

Conceal afikoman: Three pieces of unleavened bread are on the table. Break the middle piece, wrap it in a napkin, and hide it somewhere in the house.

Narration: Tell the story of the Exodus.

The "Dayenu" song: Sing a song to remind the guests about the gifts the Lord has given. After each blessing say "Dayenu," which means "it would have been enough for us."

Second cup: Bless the second cup of juice.

Questions of a child and symbolism: The youngest child asks questions about the meal. The leader explains the special food symbols on the Passover plate: unleavened bread, bitter herbs, charoset, lamb bone, parsley, and egg.

Meal: Bless, serve, and eat the meal.

Find afikoman: The children search for the hidden bread wrapped in a napkin. The finder brings it to the table and receives a prize. Everyone eats a piece of the afikoman.

---

1. Pronounced ha-ga-DAH. Haggadah means "the telling." It is the script that is read at the Passover dinner.

Praise: Recite psalms of praise.

Third cup: Bless the third cup of juice.

Inviting Elijah: Pour a cup of juice for the prophet Elijah. Open the door and invite him into the home.

Fourth cup: Bless the fourth cup of juice. The text ends with the phrase "Next year in Jerusalem! Next year may all be free!"

Hymn: Conclude the service by singing a hymn.

PART ONE: BEFORE THE MEAL

INSTRUCTIONS: The following text is an authentic Jewish Haggadah, to which additions have been made to make the Passover feast appropriate for Latter-day Saint participants. The Mormon-oriented additions to the script are printed in *italics,* so they can be easily identified. These interpretive passages, obviously, are not part of the authentic Jewish service.

Throughout the script, sub-titles have been used to introduce the various sections of the Passover meal. They are placed for the reader's convenience, but they should not be read to the group.

In performing this script, the Introduction, the Exodus story, and the Conclusion, should be ready by the leader. The remaining quotations and prayers may be read either by the leader or by other participants who the leader assigns prior to the presentation.

Sentences indicating an action to be performed have been underlined. They are part of the spoken script and should be read or spoken to the group.

Other instructions which indicate or describe various actions will also be underlined, but they will be placed in square brackets [ ], indicating that they are not to be read to the group.

Introduction[2]

For members of The Church of Jesus Christ of Latter-day Saints, Easter is the holiest day of the year. It is a day set aside to honor the resurrection of Jesus Christ and the subsequent hope we have for eternal life. This joyous news has been celebrated for thousands of years—long before Jesus came to Earth. Centuries before his mortal ministry, Jesus was known as the great Jehovah, Creator of the heavens and the earth, the God of the Old Testament. Since the days of Adam, God taught his children to look forward to the time when Christ would come. Our Eternal Father gave us commandments and stories that symbolized the redemption that would be possible because of His holy Son.

One ancient prophet wrote, "For this intent have we written these things, that [you] may know that we knew of Christ, and we had a hope of his glory many hundred years before his coming; and not only we ourselves had a hope of his glory, but also all the holy prophets which were before us. Behold, they believed in Christ and worshiped the Father in his name, and also we worship the Father in his name. And for this intent we keep the law of Moses, it pointing our souls to him."[3]

Tonight we have gathered as family and friends to observe one of the ancient ceremonies that taught our ancestors of Christ. It is called Passover. It is still observed by faithful Jews all over the world. Although we understand the symbols differently than they do, we believe that we truly worship the

---

2. The Passover leader reads the Introduction, the Exodus story, and the Conclusion. The remaining quotes and prayers may be read by any of the participants.

3. Jacob 4:4-11.

same God. May we someday all celebrate together with the Messiah in peace and love. This is our prayer.

Lighting the Candles

We will begin by asking _____ to light the candles.

[Two white candles are now lit, traditionally by the matriarch of the family. Using both hands, she draws the warmth towards her face and says the prayer:]

Blessed art Thou, O Lord our God, Ruler of the universe who sanctifies us with commandments and asks us to kindle the lights of the festival. Blessed art Thou, O Lord our God, Ruler of the universe, who has given us life and allows us to celebrate this joyous occasion.[4]

Historical Introduction

The history of our people reaches back to the beginning of time. Once we were slaves in the land of Egypt, but today we are free. Long ago, on a night such as this, our ancestors went forth out of Egypt, leaving behind slavery and degradation. On a night such as this they rejoiced in their newfound freedom. Tonight we celebrate their freedom and ours. But we remember that there is still slavery in this world, both physical and spiritual. May this holy day inspire us to share the light of freedom with all the world.[5]

---

4. See also 3 Nephi 15:3-10; 23:5; 25:4, Alma 25:15-16, and Jacob 4:4-5.

5. All prayers were translated from the original Hebrew by Marianne Monson-Burton.

First Cup of Grape Juice

Tonight we will drink four cups of grape juice. There are many different explanations for this custom.[6] It has been said that the four cups of Passover wine (or grape juice) symbolize God's four promises to save His people: "I will bring you out . . . I will deliver you . . . I will redeem you . . . I will take you to be my people."[7]

We can also think of the four cups as representing four types of freedom. The first cup represents physical freedom, the most basic freedom of all. Without physical freedom, we do not have the ability to learn of any other freedom. When the people of Israel were in Egypt, the Egyptian rulers took away their freedom, and set taskmasters over them to afflict them with their burdens.[8]

<u>Now we will say the prayer for the grape juice:</u>

Blessed art Thou, O Lord our God, Ruler of the universe, and Creator of the fruit of the vine.

<u>Everyone may drink the first cup of grape juice.</u>

<u>Now we will pass a bowl, and pour warm water over your hands so you can wash them.</u>[9]

---

6. There are hundreds of Jewish Haggadahs, or scripts for the Passover Seder. This Seder text is not taken from one particular Haggadah, but it is typical of traditional Jewish Seder texts. The author read through many Haggadah texts and sought to remain true to the spirit and formula of the Jewish traditions.

As is generally the case with spiritual symbolism, many layers of meaning exist. Therefore, every part of the Passover has numerous possible interpretations. Encourage participants to discuss their own ideas about what this experience can teach us. A lively discussion is a traditional part of every Jewish Passover.

7. Exodus 6:6, 7.

8. Exodus 1:14.

9. *NOTE:* The leader may want to carry a pitcher of warm water, a bowl (to pour it into over each guest's hands), and a towel which the participants can use to dry their hands.

Eating Karpas:[10]
Parsley or Green Vegetable

It is springtime. A few months ago the land was covered in coldest winter. But now the sun is brighter, trees are blooming, and flowers are opening. Out of the death that is winter, life has begun again. The karpas reminds us that there is hope for new life, even in the midst of bondage. We dip the karpas in salt water because tears taste salty. We remember the tears our people cried in Egypt when they were slaves.

We also remember the pain and sorrow that we feel when we are in the bondage of sin. The green reminds us that in the midst of suffering, there is hope for new life and repentance because of Jesus Christ.

We will say the prayer for the Karpas:

Blessed art Thou, O Lord our God, ruler of the universe, Creator of the fruit of the earth.

Now, everyone may dip a piece of parsley in salt water and eat it.

Hiding the Afikoman[11]

There are three matzot[12] on the Passover table. We now will break the middle matzah and wrap a piece of it in a napkin. We will hide this piece away, and it will be called the afikoman. Later we will share this bread together.

The matzah is the bread of suffering that our people ate when they were slaves in Egypt. We invite all who are hungry to join us. We pray that all in bondage will soon be free.

---

10. Pronounced car-PAS.
11. Pronounced ah-fe-CO-mun.
12. The plural is MAH-ts-ot." Singular is MAH-ts-ah.

Telling of the Story

Nearly four thousand years ago, the children of Israel were slaves in Egypt. Pharaoh forced our people to make bricks and build the pyramids. We were in the bitterest bondage, with little hope for escape, so we cried out to God for help. God heard our plea, saw our suffering, and responded to our oppression. God remembered the Covenant He made with our ancestors Abraham, Isaac, and Jacob. He called a humble shepherd named Moses to be His prophet. The Lord told Moses, "I have surely seen the affliction of my people which are in Egypt, and have heard their cry. . . . And I am come down to deliver them."[13]

Moses told Pharaoh that the Lord wanted His people to go free, but Pharaoh refused, so God brought plagues to the land of Egypt. <u>When we recall these plagues, we remove one drop of grape juice from our cups for each of the ten plagues. Remove the drop of juice with your finger and place it on your plate or in a napkin.</u>

The grape juice is our symbol of joy, and our joy is lessened when we remember that our freedom caused the suffering of God's children. We do not wish anyone to suffer, not even our enemies.

Together, let us recall the Ten Plagues against Egypt. I will say each plague and <u>you are to repeat each one after me, and remove a drop of juice for each plague</u>:

River turns to blood; [<u>repeat</u>]
Frogs upon the land; [<u>repeat</u>]
Lice in man and beast; [<u>repeat</u>]
Swarms of flies; [<u>repeat</u>]
Cattle plague; [<u>repeat</u>]

---

13. Exodus 3:7-8.

Boils breaking forth; [repeat]
Hail mingled with fire; [repeat]
Locusts covering the ground; [repeat]
And three days of darkness" [repeat].[14]

Still, Pharaoh refused to let us go. Finally, the Lord prepared his people so they would escape his last plague. He told
Israel that each family should find an unblemished lamb. The
lamb was to be sacrificed, and the blood was to be put on the
top and sides of the Israelite door frames. The Lord told them,

"The blood shall be to you for a token upon the houses
where ye are; and when I see the blood, I will pass over you,
and the plague shall not be upon you to destroy you, when I
smite the land of Egypt."[15]

That night our ancestors ate the Passover lamb with
unleavened bread and bitter herbs.

The bone[16] on our Passover plate reminds us that the angel
of death passed over the houses of our ancestors because of
the blood of the lamb. When Pharaoh's own son died, he
finally agreed to let us go. We remove one final drop of grape
juice from our cups for the final plague and repeat after me:
"Slaying of the firstborn." [repeat]

The Lord told Moses that the children of Israel should
remember this Passover miracle forever.[17] Four times in the
Old Testament we are commanded to teach our children about

---

14. Exodus 7-10.
15. Exodus 12:13.
16. See Exodus 12:3-11. The Hebrew word for the lamb bone on
the Passover plate is "Zeroah" (pronounced "zer-oh-AH").
17. See Exodus 12:14-17, 24-25, 42.
18. See Exodus 12:25-27; 12:42; 13:8; 13:14.

the miraculous deliverance that God provided.[18] And so today we teach our children this humbling story.

And as we tell this story, we realize that Easter is actually the same celebration as Passover. They both remind us that freedom from spiritual bondage is bought "with the precious blood of Christ, as of a lamb without blemish and without spot: who verily was foreordained before the foundation of the world."[19] The firstborn children of the Israelites were spared, but God's own firstborn would not be.

One of our apostles, Elder Bruce R. McConkie, wrote that "They were to take of the blood of the lamb and sprinkle it upon the doorposts of their houses, having this promise as a result: 'and the blood shall be to you for a token upon the houses where ye are: and when I see the blood, I will pass over you, and the plague shall not be upon you to destroy you,' signifying that the blood of Christ, which should fall as drops in Gethsemane and flow in a stream from a pierced side as he hung on the cross, would cleanse and save the faithful; and that, as those in Israel were saved temporally because the blood of a sacrificial lamb was sprinkled on the door posts of their houses, so the faithful of all ages would wash their garments in the blood of the Eternal Lamb, and from him receive an eternal salvation."[20]

It Would Have Been Enough

God has done wonderful things for us. He gave us life; He delivered us from bondage, both physical and spiritual; He gave us the Sabbath and the holy scriptures. As we ponder all that the Lord has done for us, we are overwhelmed with His goodness and mercy. Every blessing fills our hearts with joy

---

19. 1 Peter 1:19-20.
20. McConkie, *Promised Messiah*, 426.

and gratitude; therefore, for each blessing we say "Dayenu," [pronounced di-AY-nu] which means, "It would have been enough for us."

I will recount some of the blessings God has given to his people. After each blessing, let us say together, "Dayenu":

Had God only given us life, <u>Dayenu</u>.
Had God only brought us out of Egypt, <u>Dayenu</u>.
Had God only led us through the desert, <u>Dayenu</u>.
Had God only brought us to the land of Israel, <u>Dayenu</u>.
Had God only given us the Sabbath, <u>Dayenu</u>.
Had God only given us the scriptures, <u>Dayenu</u>.
Had God only given us the Temple, <u>Dayenu</u>.
Had God only sent us prophets, <u>Dayenu</u>.
Had God only given us freedom, <u>Dayenu</u>.

[<u>More blessings, unique to the group, may be added here by the Leader</u>], <u>Dayenu</u>.

Second Cup of Grape Juice

The second cup of grape juice symbolizes intellectual freedom—freedom of the mind. Closed minds lead to misunderstanding and human suffering, but truth leads to greater freedom and tolerance for everyone.

"The glory of God is intelligence, or in other words, light and truth. Light and truth forsake that evil one. He that keepeth [God's] commandments receiveth truth and light, until he is glorified in truth and knoweth all things."[21]

[<u>The juice is again served into everyone's cup.</u>]

<u>We will say the prayer for the grape juice:</u>

Blessed art Thou, O Lord our God, ruler of the universe, Creator of the fruit of the vine.

<u>Everyone may drink the second cup of grape juice.</u>

---

21. D&C 93:28, 36, 37).

Questions of a Child

The Lord has commanded us to teach our children the stories of the scriptures. God loves little children and wants us all to be more like them. With innocence and trusting, a small child accepts the gospel in perfect faith. Children love to ask questions, and they should be encouraged to ask. We learn so much from the questions of a child.[22]

<u>Now a child asks:</u> "Why do we eat matzah tonight?"

Tonight we eat the matzah because the Jews left Egypt in such a hurry that they did not have time to let their bread dough rise. They baked it immediately and it came out flat and hard—the first matzah.[23] This unleavened bread can remind us of purity; it is free from the leaven of sin.

The matzah also reminds us of our Savior, who is the pure bread of life. Surely he sustains us in the wilderness of life, just as manna sustained our ancestors in the desert.

<u>We will say the prayer over the matzah:</u>

Blessed art Thou, O Lord our God, ruler of the universe, who sanctifies us with commandments and asks us to eat matzah.

<u>Everyone may eat a piece of matzah.</u>

---

22. In the traditional Jewish Passover, a child asks about why Passover night is different from all other nights. (Usually we eat bread, why tonight do we eat only unleavened bread?) These questions are answered, and then the leader talks about four different kinds of children (wise, wicked, simple, and unable to ask). After the telling of the Exodus story, the meanings of the bone, matzah, and maror are explained. I have simply combined these two portions of the Haggadah so that the children ask about the symbolism of the items on the Passover plate. This was done to give more clarity for an LDS audience less familiar with the items.

23. See Exodus 12:8, 33-34, 39.

Now a child asks: "Why do we eat bitter herbs tonight?"

The bitter herbs[24] remind us of the pain and bitterness of slavery. If Israel had not been redeemed, you and I would still be enslaved today. In every generation, each of us should feel as though we ourselves had gone forth from Egypt, as it is written, "you shall explain to your child on that day, it is because of what God did for me when *I myself* went forth from Egypt."[25] So at Passover we each personally experience the bitterness of bondage and the joy of deliverance.

In much the same way, the atonement must be personally accepted. We know that the Savior suffered for us as individuals. We must apply its message of freedom to our own lives.

Remember, "He was wounded for our transgressions, he was bruised for our iniquities; the chastisement of our peace was upon him; and with his stripes we are healed."[26]

We will say the prayer for the bitter herbs:

Blessed art Thou, O Lord our God, ruler of the universe, who sanctifies us with commandments and asks us to eat Maror.

Everyone may eat a bitter herb.

Now a child asks: "Why do we eat charoset[27] tonight?"

Charoset is a mixture of fruit, nuts, and honey that reminds us of the mortar the Jewish slaves used to assemble Pharaoh's

---

24. See Exodus 12:8. The Hebrew word for the bitter herbs is "maror" (pronounced mah-ROAR).

25. Deuteronomy 6:20.

26. Isaiah 53:5.

27. Pronounced chare-OH-set. The beginning "ch" is the guttural Hebrew letter "chet." We have no corresponding sound in English, but it is similar to the French "R."

bricks, when the Egyptians "made their lives bitter with hard bondage, in mortar, and in brick, and in all manner of service in the field: all their service, wherein they made them serve, was with rigour."[28]

The charoset is sweet, reminding us of the sweetness of hope for redemption. We eat the bitter herbs of slavery together with the charoset and matzah of freedom. This is because in the time of slavery there is always hope for release. In times of freedom, there is always the memory of slavery.

The beautiful parallel is that when we are in the midst of sin, we have hope for forgiveness because of Christ. When we are clean, we remember the pain of the past, and we know it is Jesus' sacrifice that made it possible for our burden to be lifted.

"He hath sent me to bind up the brokenhearted, to proclaim liberty to the captives, and the opening of the prison to them that are bound. . . . to give unto them beauty for ashes, the oil of joy for mourning."[29]

Everyone may eat bitter herbs, and charoset, on a piece of matzah.

Now a child asks: "Why do we eat an egg[30] tonight?"

The roasted egg represents the Passover sacrifice made in the ancient Temple in Jerusalem. An egg also reminds us of the circle of life out of death.

When the egg is dipped in salt water, we can remember that the miracle of resurrection came through the tears of our Savior.

---

28. Exodus 1:14.
29. Isaiah 61:1, 3.
30. The Hebrew word for the egg is "beytzah" (pronounced bay-TSAH).

"For he said, Surely they are my people, children that will not lie: so he was their Savior. In all their affliction he was afflicted, and the angel of his presence saved them: in his love and in his pity he redeemed them; and he bare them, and carried them all the days of old."[31]

Everyone may eat a slice of egg dipped in salt water.

PART TWO:
THE MEAL IS SERVED AND EATEN

We will pass a bowl of water so that you all may wash your hands. [Pass the bowl and wait until all hands are washed.]

We will say the blessing on the meal:

Blessed art Thou, O Lord our God, Ruler of the universe, who brings forth bread from the Earth; who sanctifies us with commandments and asks us to wash our hands. [Other words may be added to personalize the blessing to fit the needs and circumstances of the group.]

The meal will now be served. [Serve and enjoy the meal together.]

PART THREE:
THE SERVICE AFTER THE MEAL

The Afikoman

It is time for the children to search for the hidden afikoman until it is found. They will bring it back to the table, and the child who finds it will receive a small prize.[32] [The children

---

31. Isaiah 63:8-9.

32. Pronounced a-fee-KO-mun. In some traditions, *all* children who search receive a prize.

are sent to go and search, returning after the afikoman is found. The finder is praised and given the prize.]

This afikoman is a sign that what is broken off is not really lost to our people, so long as our children remember and search. Our hope is in our children: to find what is lost, to bring together what is broken, to restore our faith.

I will now break and distribute the afikoman for everyone to eat. Nothing else is eaten after the afikoman.

We can think of this afikoman as being the gospel of Christ, broken and hidden away. In future generations, children will accept the gospel and share it with their ancestors through temple ordinances. Our hope is that our children will cherish this gospel and share it with all people.

We can also think of the afikoman as the body of Christ, broken on the cross and hidden in a tomb. It remained there for three days, but on Easter morn, the Savior overcame the bonds of death. Because of his triumph, every person who has ever lived, or ever will live on this earth, will be resurrected.

President Gordon B. Hinckley once wrote, "The empty tomb that first Easter morning brought the most comforting assurance that can come into man's heart. This is the assurance of Easter. This is the promise of the risen Lord. This is the relevance of Jesus to a world in which all must die. But there is a further and more immediate relevance. As he is the conqueror of death, so also is he the master of life. His way is the answer to the troubles of the world in which we live."[33]

---

33. Gordon B. Hinckley, "The Wonder of Jesus," *Improvement Era,* June 1969, 74.

Praise the Lord

In gratitude and humility, we all say "Halleluiah,"[34] which means "Praise the Lord." It is customary to have a reading selected from Psalms 116 through 118. These psalms are songs of praise. _____ will read Psalm 116, verses 3 through 5, and verse 16:

> The sorrows of death compassed me, and the pains of hell had hold of me: I found trouble and sorrow. Then called I upon the name of the Lord; O Lord, I beseech thee, deliver my soul. Gracious is the Lord, and righteous; yea, our God is merciful. . . . O Lord, truly I am thy servant; I am thy servant, and the son of thine handmaid: thou hast loosed my bonds."

Third Cup of Grape Juice

The third cup of grape juice symbolizes spiritual freedom. Our people have known the need for spiritual redemption in many ages. The prophet Daniel was forbidden by Darius, the King of the Medes, to call upon his God. But Daniel did not fear man more than God, and he continued to pray to the Almighty. The Lord protected Daniel in the depths of the lions' den.[35]

[At this point in the Seder it is customary to tell stories about modern-day threats to freedom. Often Jews recount stories from the Holocaust. You may choose to invite stories

---

34. "Halleluiah" is a transliteration from the Hebrew words "Hallel," or "praise," and the sacred name of deity in the Old Testament. This name is often transliterated into English as "Jehovah," but it was changed in the King James Bible to "LORD" (all capitalized) out of respect and because of the ancient Jewish tradition that the holy name of God should not be spoken. Therefore, "Halleluiah" literally means "Praise Jehovah."

35. See Daniel, chapter 6.

from current events or from LDS history to be shared or skip this point and move on beyond this page to where the Last Supper is explained.]

In this dispensation, our Latter-day Saint people were driven from their homes time and again because of their beliefs. Many of our ancestors walked across the plains to Utah, leaving behind physical possessions as well as the graves of their loved ones. We know personally the importance of spiritual tolerance. Today we thank God that we can worship in peace.[36]

"We claim the privilege of worshipping Almighty God according to the dictates of our own conscience, and allow all men the same privilege, let them worship how, where or what they may."[37]

But there is another spiritual freedom that we remember today. Our minds turn back to a very special Passover meal celebrated over two thousand years ago.[38] *That night, in an upper room in Jerusalem, Jesus broke unleavened bread and blessed wine as part of the Passover feast, just as we have done today. But as Jesus passed the matzah, he taught the disciples about the* **original** *significance of the emblems. Of the broken bread he said, "Take, eat; this is my body." Of the wine he said, "Drink ye all of it. For this is my blood of the new testament, which is shed for many for the remission of sins."*[39]

---

36. In keeping with this tradition, I have recalled a time of suffering and bondage from Latter-day Saint history.

37. Article of Faith 11.

38. According to Mark, Jesus used the last cup of the Seder to endow the wine with its true meaning.

39. Matthew 26:26-28.

The next day, the Lamb of God, the true Paschal lamb, was slain for the sins of the world. As Paul wrote, "Christ our passover is sacrificed for us."[40]

Because of the Savior's sacrifice, the Apostle Paul wrote that we can be "delivered from the bondage of corruption into the glorious liberty of the children of God."[41]

[The juice is again served into everyone's cup.]

We will now say the blessing on the grape juice:

Blessed art Thou, O Lord our God, ruler of the universe, Creator of the fruit of the vine.

Everyone may drink the third cup of grape juice.

Elijah's Cup

This special cup of grape juice is reserved for the prophet Elijah. The prophet Malachi[42] promised that Elijah would come back to earth to turn the hearts of parents to their children, and the hearts of children to their parents. Traditionally, the return of Elijah is an important sign of the Messianic age, a time when light and truth will return to the earth. At every Passover celebration, the door is opened to invite the spirit of Elijah to enter and herald the coming of the Messiah.

On April 3, 1836, on the same day that Jewish families around the world celebrated Passover and invited Elijah, he did in fact return. Elijah appeared to the prophet Joseph Smith in the Kirtland Temple, and there bestowed the sealing keys for this dispensation.[43] *Today we give thanks that family ties are made possible beyond the grave through the*

---

40. 1 Corinthians 5:7.
41. Romans 8:21.
42. See Malachi 4:5-6.
43. See D&C 110:13-16.

sealing powers of the priesthood revealed by Elijah. The return of Elijah truly heralded a time when light and truth was showered upon the earth.

Now I pour a cup of grape juice for Elijah. A child will open the door to invite the prophet to enter. Together we say:

"We invite the spirit of Elijah into this home and into our hearts. May our hearts be united in God's service and sanctified by His will. May our families be bound together eternally because we as parents turn to our children, and we as children, turn to our parents."

I will say each sentence, and ask you to repeat it after me:

We invite the spirit of Elijah into this home and into our hearts.   [Repeat]

May our hearts be united in God's service and sanctified by His will.   [Repeat]

May our families be bound together eternally . . .[Repeat]

because we as parents turn to our children . . .   [Repeat]

and we as children, turn to our parents.   [Repeat]

Fourth Cup of Grape Juice

As our Seder draws to an end, we take up our cups one last time. This fourth cup of juice reminds us that redemption is not yet complete. Not everyone in our world is yet free. There is still too much sorrow and despair. This fourth cup reminds us of our responsibility to be God's servants—to bring peace to those at war, food to those who hunger, and spiritual truth to those still enslaved. This is our responsibility. May we live to fulfill it.

[The juice is again served into everyone's cup.]

We will say the blessing on the grape juice:

Blessed art Thou, O Lord our God, ruler of the universe, Creator of the fruit of the vine.

<u>Everyone may drink the fourth cup of grape juice.</u>

The Easter Story

Passover is often called the "freedom festival," for it is a celebration of liberty, both spiritual and physical. Today, at Easter time, we are particularly grateful for the freedom from sin and death made possible by our Savior. We conclude by reading an account of the first Easter morning.

"Mary Magdalene, having returned, 'stood without at the sepulchre weeping.' She stooped down and looked in and up, 'saw two angels in white sitting the one at the head, and the other at the feet, where the body of Jesus had lain.' 'Woman, why weepest thou?' The angelic visitors asked. 'Because they have taken away my Lord,' she replied, 'and I know not where they have laid him.' As much as she knew about the doctrine of the resurrection; as frequently as she had heard Jesus tell that he would be crucified and rise again the third day; as great as was her faith in him and in his word—yet in the dawning light of this Easter day, the full import of the open tomb had not yet dawned within her soul.

It was then that she turned away from the tomb and saw Jesus standing and knew not that it was Jesus. He asked: 'Woman, why weepest thou? Whom seekest thou?' In her anxiety, concerned only with her own sorrow, having neither interest in nor concern about others at that moment, she supposed the speaker was the gardener. The garden tomb was empty; who but the gardener would have carried away the body of her Lord? 'Sir, if thou have borne him hence,' she pleaded, 'tell me where thou hast laid him, and I will take him away.' Though none others were available to help, yet she would do all that a mortal can to reverence a departed loved one.

Jesus said simply: 'Mary.' Mary, his beloved; he spoke her name, nothing more. It was as when the still small voice sank into the soul of Elijah; it was though the heavens had been rent and the very throne of God set forth before men; it was as though angelic choirs had sung her name—MARY! The recognition was instantaneous. Her river of tears became a sea of joy. It is he; he has risen; he lives; I love him as of old. With soul-filled exuberance she cried, 'Rabboni' —Oh, my Master!"[44]

Conclusion

This service is now concluded, its rites observed, its purposes revealed. We will continue to celebrate this freedom festival until God's plan is known in full, and God's highest blessing sealed. May God, who redeemed our ancestors from slavery and degradation, redeem all who are enslaved and bring freedom and dignity to the entire world.

Together, let us say:

"Next year in Jerusalem! Next year may all be free!"

[The group repeats:]

Next year in Jerusalem! Next year may all be free!

Jerusalem represents the holy land after the return of the Messiah, when all the Earth will dwell in joy and peace. According to the prophet Isaiah, this is when "they shall not hurt nor destroy in all my holy mountain: for the earth shall be full of the knowledge of the Lord, as the waters cover the sea."[45]

---

44. McConkie, *The Mortal Messiah*, 4:263.
45. Isaiah 11:9.

We believe that the Messiah has come once, bringing the gifts of forgiveness and resurrection into the world. We also believe that he will come again in fulfillment of prophecy. We join our Jewish brethren as they pray for this era of joy and peace:

> Therefore, let us rejoice
> At the wonder of our deliverance
> From bondage to freedom, from agony to joy,
> From mourning to festivity,
> From darkness to light,
> From servitude to redemption.
> Before God let us ever sing a new song.

It is traditional to end Passover by singing a hymn. Let's sing _____ [See Chapter 11 for a list of suggested hymns and songs.]

11
Passover Resources

Seder Songs

Singing any of the following hymns is a perfect way to end an Easter Seder.

From *The Hymn Book of The Church of Jesus Christ of Latter-day Saints:*

- Redeemer of Israel, # 6
- All Creatures of Our God and King, # 62
- Glory to God on High, # 67
- I Know that My Redeemer Lives, # 136
- He Is Risen, # 199
- Christ the Lord Is Risen Today, # 200

From *The Children's Songbook of The Church of Jesus Christ of Latter-day Saints:*

- He Sent His Son, # 34
- Did Jesus Really Live Again?, # 64
- He Died that We Might Live Again, # 65
- When He Comes Again, # 82
- The Hearts of the Children, # 92

The songs which are reproduced on the next two pages are fun Passover songs. They are perfect for families with small children. You may wish to learn and sing them.

God of Might

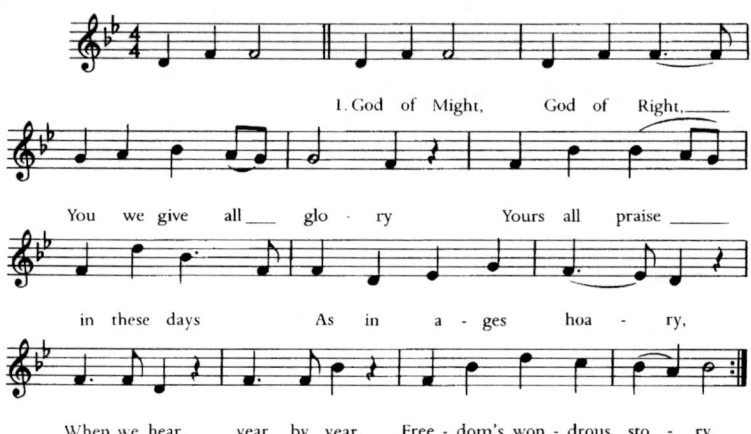

1. God of Might,   God of   Right,_____

You   we give   all___ glo · ry   Yours all   praise _____

in these days   As   in   a - ges   hoa -   ry,

When we hear,   year by year,   Free - dom's won - drous sto - ry.

2. How God gave to each slave
   Promised liberation,
   This great word Pharaoh heard
   Making proclamation:
   Set them free to serve Me
   As a holy nation.

3. We enslaved thus were saved
   Through God's might appearing,
   So we pray for the day
   When we shall be hearing
   Freedom's call reaching all,
   The people's God revering.

4. Be with all who in thrall
   To their task are driven;
   In Your power speed the hour
   When their chains are riven;
   Earth around will resound
   Joyful hymns to heaven.

Order of the Seder

Malcolm H. Stern

Babylonian Melody

1. Praise God for fruit of vine, and bless the first cup when it's time

2. In salt you dip some green. 3. Break the ma - tzah in be - tween.

3. Of three ma - tzot on the tray, take one piece to hide a - way.

4. Read how God set Is - ra - el free, res - cued us from sla - ve - ry.

5. Matzah you bless and eat.

6. With bitter herbs, haroset sweet.

7. At last the meal takes place.

8. But before you say the grace, find the afikoman.

9. Bring the supper to its end.

10. Then recite the psalms of praise, final thanks to God we raise.

The Matzah-Making Song
(sung to the tune of *Row, Row, Row Your Boat*)

Roll, roll, roll your dough
　　(rub palms together in circular motions)
Make it nice and round (pretend to form a ball)
Make it flat (slap hands together),
Poke lots of holes (pretend to poke holes in hand),
And bake it till it's brown
　　(act as if putting a tray in the oven).

Passover Song
(Sung to the tune of *London Bridge Is Falling Down*)

Moses freed the Jewish slaves,
Jewish slaves, Jewish slaves,
Moses freed the Jewish slaves,
On Passover.

He told the Pharaoh "Let them go,
Let them go, let them go,"
He told the Pharaoh "Let them go,"
On Passover.

Moses parted the Red Sea,
The Red Sea, the Red Sea,
Moses parted the Red Sea,
So they could be free.

He led them safely to the shore,
To the shore, to the shore,
He led them safely to the shore,
Slaves they are no more!

Suggestions for Using Passover in Gospel Teaching

Passover can be easily adapted for use in gospel teaching whether you are giving a sacrament meeting talk, Sunday School lesson, or fireside. Time restrictions usually do not allow for a review of the whole Seder in a teaching situation, but by carefully selecting a few areas of focus, a discussion of Passover can be an effective part of a lesson focused on the prophecies of Christ in the Old Testament.

When I teach Passover in church, I begin with scriptures testifying that the Law of Moses foreshadowed Christ's coming. I then explain that Passover is one of the ancient holidays that prepared the world for the coming of the Savior. After reviewing the story of Passover in Exodus 12, I read Exodus 12:24-25, which commands that Passover be kept forever. At this point in the lesson, you may want to ask the class why we don't fulfill this ancient command any longer. The usual response is that the holiday was fulfilled in Christ.

I explain that although this is true, Passover was so important that the Lord prepared a way for us to continue to celebrate aspects of Passover even after the Law was fulfilled. Passover celebrated freedom from bondage bought through the blood of the lamb, and Easter is really the same celebration: we celebrate the freedom from spiritual bondage and death that comes because of the blood of the Lamb of God. Because the Savior fulfilled the law with his atonement, today we celebrate Passover with its original meaning intact.

Moses and the other prophets understood the original symbolism. So did the Nephites. Other scriptures that may be helpful in this discussion include 1 Corinthians 5:7, 2 Nephi 11:4, Moses 7:47, and see the footnote at Acts 12:4. We also observe aspects of Passover each week as we partake of the sacrament. The Last Supper celebrated by Jesus and his apostles was a Passover meal, and the Savior used symbols from the Jewish feast—unleavened bread and wine—to show that Passover prophesied of his atonement.

Although we no longer celebrate Passover in its original form, there are still many truths that the ceremony can teach us. As time permits, you may want to review the possible interpretations of the symbolic foods in Chapter 4, portions of the Haggadah text in Chapter 10, Christ's celebration of Passover as the Last Supper in Chapter 5, and Elijah's return to the Kirtland Temple at Passover time in Chapter 6. Helpful visual aids for this lesson include the Passover plate with the five symbolic foods, matzah, a bottle of grape juice, and pictures of Christ (1) in Gethsemane, (2) at the Last Supper, and (3) on Resurrection morning.

Be sure to leave time for testifying of Christ, the most important part. Perhaps you will want to discuss how the Lamb of God delivered us from the bondage of sin and death. Consider discussing what the promise of resurrection means to you, and that our spirits will be united with our bodies to receive a fullness of joy. (See D&C 128:11-24 and D&C 93:33). If it is an Easter lesson, read the account of the resurrection in John 20:11-16, or the story as told by Bruce R. McConkie at the end of the Haggadah in Chapter 10.

In the years I have taught Passover in church settings, I have found that two rules are necessary to utilize Passover as an effective teaching tool:

First, it is imperative that your listeners understand that you are not suggesting that we still <u>have</u> to keep Passover today. Make sure that no one goes home thinking, *"Was*

Brother Johnson saying that we still <u>need</u> to do this?" Be very clear that Passover was fulfilled in Christ, but it is still a valuable teaching tool for us today.

Second, the focus must always be on Christ. It is easy to get caught up with the depth and meaning behind the symbols, but the point of gospel teaching is always to lead people to Christ. If it does not, the lesson has failed in its purpose. Provide enough information to illustrate the symbolism of Passover and then tie it to the Savior.

If students are interested in learning more about Passover, recommend this book! Certainly you don't need to cover every element of Passover for your lesson to be a success; nothing could be further from the truth. Although most people are very interested in learning about the festival, above all they want to feel the Spirit and understand how it is related to Christ.

Sources Consulted

Books

Bandstra, Barry L. *Reading the Old Testament: An Introduction to the Hebrew Bible.* Belmont, WA: Wadsworth Publishing, 1995.

Bradshaw, Paul F., and Lawrence A. Hoffman, eds. *Passover and Easter: Origin and History to Modern Times.* vol. 5 of Two Liturgical Traditions. Notre Dame: University of Notre Dame Press, 1999.

Brontstein, Herbert, and Leonard Baskin. *A Passover Haggadah.* New York: Central Conference of American Rabbis, 1994.

Edersheim, Alfred. *Sketches of Jewish Social Life.* New York: Eerdmans, 1976.

Fox, Rabbi Karen L., and Phyllis Zimbler Miller. *Seasons for Celebration: A Contemporary Guide to the Joys, Practices, and Traditions of the Jewish Holidays.* New York: Penguin Putnam, 1992.

Hales, Janet, and Joe Hales. *A Christ-centered Easter: Day-by-day Activities to Celebrate Easter Week.* Salt Lake: Deseret Book Co., 2002.

McConkie, Bruce R. *The Millennial Messiah: The Second Coming of the Son of Man.* Salt Lake City: Deseret Book Co., 1982.

_____. *The Mortal Messiah: from Bethlehem to Calvary.* Salt Lake City: Deseret Book Co., 1980.

_____. *The Promised Messiah: The First Coming of Christ.* Salt Lake City, Deseret Book Co., 1978.

Segal, Eliezer Lorne. *Uncle Eli's Special-for-kids, Most-Fun-Ever, Under-the-Table Passover Haggadah.* San Francisco: No Starch Press, 1999.

Smith, Joseph F. *Teachings of the Prophet Joseph Smith.* Salt Lake City: Deseret Book Co., 1976.

_____. *Doctrines of Salvation: Sermons and Writings of Joseph Fielding Smith.* 3 vols. Salt Lake City: Bookcraft, 1992.

Stallings, Joseph. *Rediscovering Passover: A Complete Guide for Christians.* San Jose: Resource Publications, 1995.

Steingroot, Ira. *Keeping Passover: Everything You Need to Know to Bring the Ancient Tradition to Life and Create Your Own Passover Celebration.* San Francisco: HarperCollins, 1995.

Talmage, James E. *Jesus the Christ: A Study of the Messiah and His Mission.* Salt Lake City: Deseret Book Co., 1982.

Wiesel, Elie and Mark Podwal. *A Passover Haggadah.* New York: Simon and Schuster, 1993.

Wilson, Marvin R. *Our Father Abraham: Jewish Roots of the Christian Faith.* Eerdmans, 1989.

Wouk, Herman. *This is My God: the Jewish Way of Life.* New York: Simon and Schuster,1986.

Wylen, Stephen M. *The Jews in the Time of Jesus.* New York: Paulist Press, 1996.

Web Sites

www.holidays.net/passover

www.kosher4passover.com

www.passover.net

www.kidsdomain.com/holiday/passover

www.deseretbook.com/mormon-life

Magazine Articles

Adams, William James Jr. "The 15th of Nisan." *Ensign,* January 1977, 45.

Banks, Ann H. "Family Easter Traditions." *Ensign,* April 1982, 12.

Benson, Ezra Taft. "A Message to Judah from Joseph." *Ensign,* December 1976, 67.

Eyring, Henry B. "Finding Safety in Counsel." *Ensign,* May 1997, 24.

Hinckley, Gordon B. "The Wonder of Jesus." *Improvement Era,* June 1969, 74.

Holland, Jeffrey R. "This Do in Remembrance of Me." *Ensign,* November 1995, 68.

Hunter, Howard W. "Christ, Our Passover." *Ensign,* May 1985, 17.

_____. "His Final Hours." *Ensign,* May 1974, 17.

Madsen, Ann N., and Barnard N. Madsen. "Judah through the Centuries." *Ensign,* January 1982, 20.

Pratt, John P. "Passover—Was it Symbolic of His Coming?" *Ensign,* January 1994, 38.

_____. "The Restoration of Priesthood Keys on Easter 1836, Part 2." *Ensign,* July 1985, 55.

Read, Lenet H. "Symbols of the Harvest: Old Testament Holy Days and the Lord's Ministry." *Ensign,* January 1975, 32.

Skousen, Cleon W. "The Old Testament Speaks Today." *Ensign,* December 1972, 79.

Treseder, Terry W. "Passover Promises Fulfilled in the Last Supper." *Ensign,* April 1990, 19.

Valletta, Thomas R. "The True Bread of Life." *Ensign,* March 1999, 7.

"Israel's Foods and Festivals," *Friend,* April 1974, 23.

Index

A

Afikoman—25, 49, 65, 131, 138.

B

Babylon—44.
Bitter herbs—63, 136.

C

Children—25, 106, 134.
Covenant—33.

E

Easter—16, 23, 24, 89.
Elijah—26, 55, 94, 141.

F

Firstborn—31.

H

Haggadah—36, 39, 52, 56, 105, 126.
Hyssop—48, 86.

J

Josiah—72, 92.

L

Lamb—23, 34, 50, 65, 83, 85, 113, 124, 133.
Law—22.

M

Manna—70.

About the Author

Marianne Monson-Burton grew up in Naperville, Illinois, the oldest of five children. She has wanted to be an author since she learned how to write. She spent six months studying at BYU's Jerusalem Center for Near Eastern Studies, and continued studying the Hebrew Bible after returning to Provo. She graduated with University Honors in English Literature from Brigham Young University.

Following graduation, she worked as Managing Editor at Beyond Words Publishing. Sister Monson-Burton has published books for children, articles in the *Ensign* magazine, and she teaches writing classes at Portland Community College.

Sister Monson-Burton has been accepted into Hebrew Bible graduate programs at Harvard, Brandeis, and the University of Chicago, but plans to defer this experience for a few years as she pursues an honorary degree in "domestic engineering" instead.

In the Church she has served as gospel doctrine teacher, primary chorister, and ward missionary. In addition to writing, her favorite activities include traveling, painting, reading, and playing fun games with her children. She lives in Hillsboro, Oregon with her husband, Keith, son Nathanael, and daughter Aria Lynn.